Ways of Sunlight

Samuel Selvon

With a critical introduction by Jane Grant

 LONGMAN

Addison Wesley Longman Limited,
Edinburgh Gate, Harlow, Essex CM20 2JE, England
and Associated Companies throughout the world.

Carlong Publishers (Caribbean) Ltd,
P. O. Box 489, Kingston 10,
33 Second Street, Newport West,
Kingston 13, Jamaica

Lexicon Trinidad Ltd,
Boundary Road, San Juan,
Trinidad, West Indies

Copp Clark Longman, 2775 Matheson Blvd East,
Mississauga, Ontario L4W 4P7

Longman Publishers USA
10 Bank Street, White Plains,
New York 10601-1951, USA

First published by MacGibbon and Kee 1957
First published in Longman Caribbean Writers series 1985
Reprinted with introduction 1987
Eighteenth impression 1997

Produced by Longman Asia Limited, Hong Kong.
PPLC/18

ISBN 0 582 64261 2

Contents

Introduction

The author

Samuel Selvon was born in Trinidad in 1923 of East Indian parents. He served as a wireless operator with the Royal Naval Reserve during the war and worked as a journalist on the *Trinidad Guardian* before turning to imaginative fiction. A number of his short stories and poems were published in the important Barbadian magazine *Bim* and in other literary magazines and he also sub-edited the *Guardian Weekly,* which was devoted to Caribbean prose and poetry. His early writing success in Trinidad encouraged him, like so many other West Indian writers of the same generation, to go to Britain to establish himself as a writer. His friend, the Barbadian novelist George Lamming, who travelled on the same ship with him to Britain in 1950, tells us (in the chapter 'Journey to an Expectation' in his book *The Pleasures of Exile*) that Selvon's first novel was already almost completed by the time he left Trinidad. *A Brighter Sun* was the first of the new wave of West Indian novels to be published in the 1950s, appearing in London in 1952. Selvon then went on to establish himself as a prolific and distinguished writer, not just of novels and short stories but also of radio and television plays and even filmscripts. Over the years he has received a number of literary awards and fellowships in recognition of his work.

Samuel Selvon's published work so far falls into two main categories: the 'Trinidad' novels and the 'London' novels – with the short story collection *Ways of Sunlight* and his new novel *Moses Migrating* very effectively linking the two. Selvon lived for twenty-eight years in London (with a few visits back to the West Indies) but in 1978 moved to Canada. He claims that he wanted to get back to the Western hemisphere and enjoys the 'new world feeling' of Canada, compared with the 'old world feeling' of Britain.[1] He claims that he hopes eventually to write a 'West Indian view of life in Canada' but his latest novel *Moses Migrating* is set in both London and Trinidad.

Background to *Ways of Sunlight* and Selvon's other work

All Samuel Selvon's novels set in Trinidad revolve around the East Indian community of which he and his fellow-Trinidadian novelist V.S. Naipaul were members. This community has its origins in the indentured labour scheme under which about 143,000 indentured labourers were transported to Trinidad from the Indian sub-continent between the years 1845 and 1917 to work on the sugar estates. Some of these labourers returned to India but most remained and their descendants now form about half of the total population of Trinidad.

The conditions under which indentured labourers lived were undoubtedly very harsh in the early years. But there was never the same systematic attempt to destroy the culture and traditions of the Indians as there had been to destroy the African culture of the slaves. Partly for this reason, and also because the Indians tended to remain in self-contained family groups and villages in the countryside (often continuing to work on the sugar estates), many have managed to retain their culture and traditions – in food, dress, religion, even language – to a quite remarkable degree. However, in recent years as more have moved to the towns, younger East Indians in particular have tended to become more 'creolised', that is to identify increasingly with Trinidad rather than with an India most will never see. Selvon himself fits into this 'creolised' category. He writes: 'I never grew up with any Indian traditions or customs, but rather as a "Trinidadian", living among people of various nationalities and imbibing "western" culture.'

[1]See interview with Susheila Nasta on 'The Moses Trilogy' in the ATCAL journal *Wasafiri*, Vol. 1 No.2, Spring 1985 p.9.

In Selvon's Trinidad books we see both sides of East Indian life: the close-knit, almost exclusively Indian village communities in the countryside and the more open, less rigid lives of Indians in the urban and suburban areas. The first of these books, *A Brighter Sun* (1952), centres around the young East Indian boy Tiger growing up in the Trinidad of the Second World War. It opens with Tiger's marriage at the age of sixteen to his child-bride Urmilla and follows his attempts to establish himself away from the influence of his family. We see Tiger undergoing the same process of 'creolisation' which was happening to so many other East Indians at the time. When the Americans build a road through the suburb of Port of Spain where he lives, Tiger abandons his garden to work on the road but he remains constantly obsessed with worries about what he should do with his life. In the sequel to this book, *Turn Again, Tiger* (1958), he returns with Urmilla and their daughter to help his father in the canefields in the country. Both books convey a powerful, authentic picture of a peasant, or near peasant, community still living a close, cohesive life close to the land.

In 1955 Selvon had published another book, *An Island is a World*. Most of the action of this novel is also set in Trinidad, but it is a much less successful novel, lacking the cohesion and 'rooted' quality of the Tiger books. Selvon's friend George Lamming has commented that, like the Jamaican writer Vic Reid, Selvon is essentially a peasant himself and in this lies his power as a novelist: 'I don't care what jobs they did before; what kind or grade of education they got in their different islands; they never really left the land that once claimed their ancestors like trees.'[2] In fact Selvon did not come from a rural background himself but he was close enough to such communities to observe them closely and certainly most people seem agreed that Selvon's most successful novels are those that deal with simple, working people whether in Trinidad or London. His next Trinidad novel, for instance, *I Hear Thunder* (1963) revolves around a middle-class group of

[2]George Lamming, *The Pleasures of Exile*, London: Michael Joseph, 1960 p.45.

Trinidadians of all races and colours and once again totally lacks the powerful 'rooted' quality of the Tiger novels.

But there is another problem which confronted Selvon and his fellow West Indian writers living in London (and indeed any writer living in exile from his native land). It is obviously much easier to write about a place when the experience is fresh in your mind and the powerful quality of the Tiger books must owe much to the fact that they were written either in, or within a few years of leaving, Trinidad. Selvon himself talked about this problem when, on his first visit home in 1963, he told the *Trinidad Guardian:* 'I do not think I could have written another book set in the West Indies without coming back to live among my people again.' But in fact his visits home have been neither very long nor very frequent. During his longest visit in 1969, when he stayed for at least six months, he was to write *The Plains of Caroni* which was published in 1970. This is his only book to be completely written in Trinidad and certainly succeeds in giving an extremely interesting picture of the complexities of Trinidadian life in the post-Independence era. But his next Trinidad book, *Those Who Eat the Cascadura* (1972), is less successful. In it he again attempts to depict a simple, peasant community but the result utterly lacks the authentic power of the Tiger books and instead gives an over-romanticised, almost sentimental, view of peasant life.

It was hardly surprising that Selvon found it hard to reproduce the life of the Trinidadian peasant after more than twenty years in London and, apart from *A Brighter Sun*, his most successful books are generally thought to be those set in London. *The Lonely Londoners* (1956) tells the story of a group of young West Indian men (or 'boys' as Selvon calls them) trying to establish themselves in the London of the early 1950s. It is interesting that, while Selvon's Trinidad books are mainly set in East Indian communities, the London books revolve around groups of West Indian friends of all races and shades.

The Lonely Londoners is very loose and episodic in structure

— more of a 'ballad' than a straight novel — but in so far as it has a plot it revolves around Moses Allotea, an early arrival in London, who acts as a central point in the book and whose room remains one of the few spots that bring the 'boys' together. The group of friends experience considerable difficulty both in finding and keeping jobs and in finding places to live. They also find the English winter and, still more, the hostility of the English people hard to cope with. (The 1950s was a period of mass West Indian immigration into Britain and many English people felt their jobs and chances of getting a house were threatened.) Nevertheless, in spite of all the difficulties, this is an extremely funny book; the exploits of Sir Galahad, Cap, Tolroy, Moses and others all make uproarious reading although, as Moses comments at the end, often 'they only laughing because they fraid to cry'.

The boys in *The Lonely Londoners* may spend a lot of their time pursuing girls but this is a society of mainly single men; there are few families and no children. By *The Housing Lark*, published almost ten years later in 1965, things are changing. The Commonwealth Immigrants Act had been passed in 1962. This act seriously limited the number of new arrivals and most of those who did now arrive were women and children joining men already settled in Britian. So what we tend to find in this period is a process whereby the West Indians begin to settle down and establish themselves as a *community* in the true sense of the word. The boys in *The Housing Lark*, for instance, (they are not actually the same characters as in the earlier book but their way of life is very similar) are still living in appalling housing conditions, at the mercy of unscrupulous landlords, but they are no longer prepared to put up with these conditions for ever. Encouraged by a new arrival from Jamaica, Harry Banjo, they start a fund to buy a house. It all starts as a 'lark'. But then the women step in and start getting things organised. By the end it seems as if the two room-mates, Battersby and Harry, will be forced to become respectable married men and that the house will eventually be bought, whatever the difficulties. In other words, a definite process of 'settling down' is taking place.

Selvon's next book about life in London, *Moses Ascending*, was published ten years later again, in 1975. In this book Selvon returns to the characters of *The Lonely Londoners* who are now, like himself, in middle-age. Tolroy has returned to Jamaica selling his house to Moses who, after twenty years in basement rooms, now proudly establishes himself in the 'penthouse' at the top of the house with an English servant Bob, whom he ironically calls his 'Man Friday', to look after him. But Moses finds himself out of tune with the new generation of young blacks in London, especially the Black Power movement which his old friend Sir Galahad has joined with enthusiasm. He also gets into deep trouble when he discovers a mysterious tenant is using his house as a staging post for importing illegal immigrants from Pakistan and by the end of the book Moses's luck has turned completely — he is back in the basement!

In these three books, spanning nearly twenty years, Selvon has managed to give us a very funny but also very perceptive and revealing picture of what life has been like for West Indians in London.

His latest book, *Moses Migrating* (1983), shows Moses deciding to return to Trinidad, although he is careful not to sell his house in London. Ironically he feels no more at home in Trinidad than in London, spending much of his time in the Hilton Hotel with his white friends. He sees his main purpose in Trinidad to show that Britain is not finished and wins prizes for his creation of 'Britannia' in Carnival. But this book too ends in disillusionment. Moses returns to London and both he and the reader are left at the airport to wonder whether the country he has so loyally defended will in fact allow him to re-enter.

Ways of Sunlight

This book of short stories is particularly interesting because it brings together within one cover the two different settings for Selvon's writing — Trinidad and London. It was first published in 1957, a year after *The Lonely Londoners* and five years after *A Brighter Sun*. It was also still only seven years after Selvon had left Trinidad (and many of the stories were written much earlier) so that he is still in this book sufficiently close to the experience of life in Trinidad to record it on the whole with the sort of authenticity which we find in the Tiger books.

Of the nine stories in this Trinidad section, six are set in the country, in isolated, almost entirely East Indian communities whose ways of life had changed little over the last fifty years. These people live close to the land, are still deeply influenced by Indian religions and languages and often suspicious of outside influences, including the disruptive effects of education. But many of the younger members are already in the process of becoming educated and we see the disruption this can cause in a story like 'Cane is Bitter' where the schoolboy son of peasant parents returns home.

This is a way of life which seems increasingly threatened, especially by the changes brought about by the Second World War and the influx of Americans into Trinidad. In the three remaining stories we move out of these self-enclosed communities into the less restricted life of the towns of Trinidad and beyond, where change has been far more rapid.

In the London section of this book we move further still — with characters who come not only from Trinidad but from all over the West Indies — across the Atlantic to London. This section shows the 'boys' leading much the same lives as the characters in *The Lonely Londoners*, adapting both their language and their way of life to their new environment, although some seem a little more settled in their jobs than in the earlier book and Brackley (in 'Brackley and the Bed') is already finding himself forced into marriage. They also seem to be establishing better relationships with the English people with whom they come in contact (usually at work). It should be pointed out however that this is the 1950s: the position for black people in England today is very different (as Selvon's own later work shows).

These stories are not straight reporting. They are imaginative recreations of people's lives and it is as creative literature that we enjoy them.

Many reviewers have commented on the episodic nature of Selvon's books, particularly those set in London, and Selvon himself repeatedly refers to them as written in 'ballad' style, closely related to the calypsonian ballads which were so popular in Trinidad at the time. This loose conversational style makes Selvon a natural story-teller and some of these short stories are amongst the best things he has ever written. Many of them are also, like his London novels, very funny, although once more there is usually sadness beneath the humour.

Part One: Trinidad

Johnson and the Cascadura

This story forms the basis of Selvon's much later novel *Those Who Eat the Cascadura* (1972) which again concerns the love affair between an Indian peasant girl (there called Sarojin) on a cocoa estate and a visiting Englishman, Garry. It is not Selvon's most successful novel and has been accused of giving an over-romantic, almost sentimental view of peasant life. Much the same criticisms can be made of this short story.

Those Who Eat the Cascadura ends in uncertainty. Garry goes back to England leaving Sarojin pregnant and it seems unlikely that the 'native legend' according to which:

> Those who eat the cascadura will, the native legend says,
> Wheresoever they may wander, end in Trinidad their days

will be fulfilled. This story, however, has a happy ending when Garry returns with a mysterious illness which means he has to live in the tropics. He marries Urmilla and settles down on the estate. You may feel this rather contrived ending is a further weakness in the story.

You will notice that, unlike the 'Tiger' books on life in Trinidad, Selvon makes very little use of Creole in this story. This may be another reason why this story lacks the down-to-earth, realistic quality of the 'Tiger' books.

Note: 'la diablesse' (p. 4) is a French spelling of the Creole word 'la jablesse'' meaning a female devil.

Down the Main

This story has a completely different setting and a completely different style to go with it. While 'Johnson and the Cascadura' was set in the countryside amongst a group of people little affected by the rapid changes of the mid-twentieth century, the main character in 'Down the Main' has had his life turned upside down by the Second World War from which he has just been demobilised. And although most of the action of this story does not take place in Trinidad at all, but in Venezuela, its style is typical of the calypsonian ballad style for which Selvon has become famous. The immensely popular calypsoes of the 1940s described in verse and music the sort of changes which people in Trinidad, particularly in the towns, were going through – and in doing so often made a sharp social comment on these changes. In a very similar racy language and often very similar rhythm, stories like this one describe the changing face of urban/creole life in Trinidad and beyond. You will notice that the use of Creole – or a modified form of it – extends here not only to the dialogue but to the narrative as well. (See 'Selvon's use of language' at the end of this Introduction.)

The title of this story refers to the Spanish Main – the traditional name for the mainland around the Caribbean Sea which in the sixteenth and seventeenth centuries was largely controlled by the Spanish. Modern-day Venezuela is one of these countries and the fact that so many Trinidadians ('bags of fellars', p. 28) are trying to get there reminds us that there was a considerable tradition of emigration – in search of work, money or even just excitement – from the West Indies long before the mass emigration to Britain in the 1950s with which the second half of this book is concerned.

Note: 'fo' day morning' (p. 29) means before morning or pre-dawn. 'bees' (p. 34) is a slang word short for Bolivares, the currency of Venezuela.

Holiday in Five Rivers

In this story Selvon returns to a quiet rural setting similar to that of 'Johnson and the Cascadura' where, unlike the characters in 'Down the Main', the peasants 'lived simply, out of touch with happenings in other parts of Trinidad' (p. 41). Selvon was to use the village of Five Rivers as the setting also for *Turn Again, Tiger* (1958). You will notice that the language of narration is far closer to Standard English here than in 'Down the Main'. You will also notice that, unlike the stories set in the towns, this is an almost entirely East Indian community (More Lazy and the shopkeeper Chin seem to be the only exceptions). This illustrates the point that until very recently most East Indians in Trinidad continued to live in isolated, largely self-sufficient, peasant communities in the countryside.

Cane is Bitter

This story was first published in *Bim* 13 (December 1950), so it must have been written either before Selvon left Trinidad or immediately after. It is again set in the countryside and concerns the lives of East Indian peasant workers on the Cross Crossing sugar estate. The picture of estate life seems to be presented here in a far more realistic and less romanticised way than in 'Johnson and the Cascadura' although we find that the rhythms of these simple lives are once more disrupted by the arrival of an outsider. In this case, however, the disruption comes not from a foreigner but from one of their own – Romesh, the schoolboy son of

Ramlal and Rookmin, who is returning to Cross Crossing for his school holidays. In Romesh's confused reaction to the various demands made on him Selvon gives us a very vivid picture of the dilemma facing the educated, creolised Indian from such a background. In the end Romesh rejects the fate which Tiger (in *A Brighter Sun* and *Turn Again, Tiger*) had had forced upon him – an early, arranged marriage and a life tied to hard toil on the land. He is able to escape through education but the implications are that such a fate awaits his less privileged brothers and sisters.

Note: The reference to 'governments in the West Indies ... talking about federating the islands' (p. 53) fixes this story firmly in the years leading up to the election of the first West Indian Federal Government in 1958. The reference to voting for Pragsingh on page 54 is probably to the elections for the Legislative Council held in Trinidad in 1950. V. S. Naipaul was to satirise the corruption and abuses of these elections mercilessly in his novel *The Suffrage of Elvira* (1958). The reference on page 55 to 'the square' where politicians make speeches is almost certainly Woodford Square in Port of Spain where the Trinidadian leader Dr Eric Williams held his famous political rallies which earned it the name of the 'University of Woodford Square'.

The Village Washer
Like 'Down the Main' this story shows the changes which war has brought to Trinidad, although here we see the effects of the Second World War on a far more local level in another sugar-cane hamlet.

Wartime Activities
This story starts in much the same setting as 'Cane is Bitter' and concerns a young man who tries to break away from this restricted life in the countryside when he discovers his parents are planning an arranged marriage for him. (Early arranged

marriages played an important part of East Indian life. Selvon's first novel *A Brighter Sun* starts with the arranged marriage between the sixteen-year-old Tiger and his child bride Urmilla.) This young man (who is never named although he sometimes addresses himself as 'old man') lacks the education of Romesh although, like Tiger, he borrows books and magazines and has apparently taught himself to read. He has, however, plenty of ambition and while 'Cane is Bitter' was set entirely in the countryside, most of the action of this story takes place in the towns of San Fernando and Port of Spain where the young man goes to seek his fortune. The language, too, reflects this urban/creole setting, being another example of Selvon's calypsonian 'ballad' style – with a variation of Creole used not only in the dialogue but also in the narration (with the young man as the narrator in this case). So once more we have a vivid example of the changes caused in Trinidadian society by the Second World War and the process of creolisation which results. But it is interesting to see that the 'hero' here makes a completely different decision from Romesh's in 'Cane is Bitter' and the story ends not with departure but return.

Note: The reference to 'Yankee dollar falling all about' (p. 75) indicates that American dollars were in plentiful supply in Port of Spain.

Barataria (p. 78) was the village just outside Port of Spain where Tiger lived in *A Brighter Sun* and where Selvon himself lived for a time.

Chaguaramas (p. 80) was the American base built during the Second World War.

The Mango Tree

This story is set in idyllic country surroundings – this time just outside the town of San Fernando. It is not made clear whether the principal character here is the same Ma Procop of the earlier story 'The Village Washer'; certainly both ladies have a belief in the effectiveness of obeah to protect their interests in common! Once more the use of Creole is confined almost entirely to the dialogue.

Note: 'a trysting place' (p. 89) is a rather old-fashioned expression meaning an agreed meeting place, usually a place where lovers meet.

Gussy and the Boss

This story is again, like a large part of 'Wartime Activities', set in the capital Port of Spain and shows the profound changes talking place in people's lives after the war. However the narration here is in Standard English rather than in the variety of Creole used there and this may be a deliberate attempt on the author's part to reflect the more middle-class setting of the story — although Gussy himself is not, of course, middle class. This story is also strongly critical (although the criticism is at all times implied rather than stated) of colonial and racialist attitudes in Trinidad and of the whole colonial situation whereby local businesses are taken over by foreign interests. Nor does it say much for colonialism if the sort of English people who come to the colonies only come because of 'the old fear of uncertainty and instability which had driven (them) from England' (see p. 100). There seems also to be an implied criticism of the class-ridden nature of Trinidadian society when we are told that the former employees of Industrial Corporation do not join a trade union 'because they felt that trade unions were for the poor struggling labourers and they were not of that class' (p. 95).

A Drink of Water

This story is set once more in the countryside — in the isolated village of Las Lomas — and gives a very different view of country life from the rather idyllic picture given in 'The Mango Tree'. This story shows life in the country as extremely hard and at times cruel. Perhaps the most depressing aspect is the way in which the villagers are shown to be not only at the mercy of the climate but of each other's greed as well. It is a beautifully written story with both setting and characters strongly drawn. Particularly striking is the contrast between the drought-ridden countryside at the beginning and the joyful description of the downpour of rain at the end – and the way in which the tension of waiting for rain is built up until it is released in the climax at the end.

Part Two: London

Calypso in London

We saw in the Trinidad stories with a city setting how close Selvon's language there was to the same oral tradition of the streets which found expression in the immensely popular calypsoes of the period. This story, too, is a perfect example of Selvon's calypsonian ballad style; very near the end the narrator concludes 'that is as much as I know of the ballad' (p. 118). 'Calypso in London' is in fact an adaptation of an earlier story with a Trinidadian setting called 'Calypsonian'. It is very interesting to read the two stories side by side ('Calypsonian' was published in *Bim* 17 (December 1952) and in *West Indian Stories* edited by Andrew Salkey (Faber 1960)) and to see how Selvon has modified the story and the language to make it suitable for its new London setting. In the same way West Indians like Mangohead here (who actually comes from St. Vincent although his friends Hotboy and Rahamut are from Trinidad) were forced to adapt their own language and life-style when they came to London. So although the language used here (and in most of the other London stories) still has its roots firmly in the urban/creole dialect of Port of Spain it is considerably modified by its London setting. 'Peel', 'hustle' and 'liming', for example, are common Trinidadian Creole words while 'cuppa' (short for 'cup of tea') is typical English slang (see table on 'Selvon's use of language' at the end of this Introduction).

Note: The reference to the 'Suez issue' (pp. 115 and 119) fixes this story firmly in the year 1956. In that year Egypt's leader Colonel Nasser nationalised or took over the Suez Canal (which, linking as it does the Mediterranean and Red Seas, has always been an extremely important waterway, comparable to the Panama Canal) which had previously been under the control of Britain. In retaliation Britain, under her Prime Minister Anthony Eden, invaded Egypt; but was very soon forced to withdraw and concede defeat. The whole issue became extremely controversial and for a time it was a major discussion topic in England, as this story shows.

The reference to the Cape of Good Hope is to the alternative route around the south of Africa which ships would be forced to take if the Suez Canal was closed to them.

Working the Transport

Many West Indians who came to Britain in the 1950s got jobs on the buses or the underground train system (or 'tube') in London and some were actually recruited in the West Indies to do this. To take one example, mentioned here, in 1956 London Transport (L.T. for short) sent officials to Barbados expressly to recruit staff to work on the buses. This very funny story therefore shows how West Indians were actively encouraged to come to Britain in the 1950s to work in industries and services which badly needed staff.

This story also is in 'ballad' style with the narrator speaking directly and extremely informally to the reader, almost as if he is chatting with him, with all the asides, questions and interruptions of a real conversation. It is also, like many of the London stories, full of colourful nicknames (like Small Change) — just one of the examples of Selvon's lively and imaginative use of language.

Note: 'Elephant' (p. 122) is an area in South London called the Elephant and Castle, named after a pub of the same name.

The reference to 'rock'n'roll' is to the immensely popular music of the 1950s in England, many of whose young fans were known as 'teddy' boys or girls or 'teds' for short. This was because they wore a style of dress — with long jackets, narrow trousers and thick-soled shoes for the boys — that was faintly Edwardian, i.e. similar to the fashions popular in the reign of the British King Edward VII (1901-1910).

If you had a map of the London underground system in front of you you would see that West Ruislip and Ongar (see p. 125) are the furthest points West and East respectively on the Central Line — which means Change really has caused the most substantial dislocation or chaos possible.

Waiting for Aunty to Cough

This is another very funny story which again shows how the 'boys' are adapting to life in London and even, in Brackley's case, settling down with a regular English girl-friend. It also shows how thoroughly metropolitan and urbanised they have become. In spite of the fact that many would have come from rural backgrounds in the West Indies they have now become (after, in Brackley's case, eight years in London) such complete 'city boys' that they consider even the London suburbs, where Beatrice lives, as 'behind God back' (p. 127). In fact during the 1950s a high percentage of West Indians did come — as Brackley does here — to live in a very central, if rather run-down, area of London, around Ladbroke Grove and Notting Hill Gate. Portobello Road (mentioned here on p. 127) became, and has remained, an important place to buy West Indian food and generally to keep in touch with West Indian life in London. (It would be useful to have a map of London in front of you as you read this story.)

This story is once more very much a 'ballad' (see p. 130 when the narrator remarks 'Well to get back to the heart of the ballad') although it is interesting to notice the contrast between Brackley's language and that of his English girl-friend Beatrice.

Note: 'a two and ten room' (p. 127) (in pre-decimal currency) is one costing £2 10 shillings a week in rent. The 'Arch' is Marble Arch, a prominent London landmark, and the 'Gate' refers to the area known as Notting Hill Gate. The reference to the cup of coffee is also interesting; this was a period when coffee bars were beginning to become extremely popular in London.

The reference to the 'green trains' (p. 128) is to the regular railway trains which operate out of Charing Cross and Waterloo stations mainly to carry commuters (those people who come into London each day to work) to and from their homes in southern England. Most West Indians would be far more familiar with the system of underground trains, which does not operate very many services south of the River Thames.

'hops' (p. 129) are the fruit of a plant used in the brewing of beer. They are widely grown in the county of Kent south-east of London and many Londoners, especially from the poorer East End, used traditionally to spend working holidays 'picking hops'.

The Embankment (p. 130) is the road which runs along the north bank of the River Thames in London. As the story shows, the area around Charing Cross is not the most respectable of areas, especially at night. Even today the Embankment is famous for the number of tramps and other homeless people who sleep out there in all weathers.

Kew Gardens (p. 133) are very famous botanic gardens in south London where many rare plants are grown.

Eraser's Dilemma

This is another 'ballad' and another example of life 'working the transport'. Eraser's experience here, however, is a much happier one than Change's in the earlier story although there are several indications that he does not feel completely secure in his job. Eraser, like Mangohead in 'Calypso in London', comes from St. Vincent.

Brackley and the Bed

It was of the language of this story that the West Indian critic Kenneth Ramchand was to write: 'This is as far as any West Indian author has gone towards closing the gap between the language of narration and the language of the fictional character' (see 'Note on Selvon's use of language' at the end of this Introduction) and it is another perfect example of the calypsonian ballad.

The hero here seems to be a different Brackley from the chief character of 'Waiting for Aunty to Cough'. Whereas the Brackley in that story had 'settled down' with a steady girl-friend, the Brackley here settles down still further – with a wife from his home island! In this way the story reflects what was happening in the mid-1950s when many more West Indian women and children were coming to Britain to join men who had often arrived alone several years earlier. This tended to bring to an end the less restricted, if rather lonely, lives the 'boys' had been leading previously (with plenty of 'liming' and casual relationships with girls) and we see the beginning of the formation of West Indian *families* in London. It is this process which Selvon describes in his second London novel *The Housing Lark* (1965) where a group of strong-minded West Indian women begin to get the men organised into marriage, buying a house, etc. (see page ix) — just as Teena is beginning to do with Brackley here. The reference to Robinson Crusoe (p. 139) is, of course, to Daniel Defoe's famous book. Selvon returns to this theme in his novel *Moses Ascending* (1975) when Moses ironically calls his white servant Bob his 'Man Friday'. The Robinson Crusoe theme is also an important one to other West Indian writers, particularly to the St. Lucian poet and playwright Derek Walcott.

If Winter Comes

Although Selvon's books on life in London are basically light-hearted and often very funny, we are never allowed to forget for long that the laughter covers an at times fairly grim battle for survival in what is a basically alien environment. And, as this story shows, it is in the bleak London winters, with their short days, fog and bitter cold, that the 'boys' find it hardest to survive. 'A shilling for the gas meter' (p. 144) refers to the fact that most rented rooms in London were fitted with gas meters which only supplied gas for heating and cooking when 'fed' with coins.

Note: The narrator's use of the French patois word 'oui' and Brakes's use of the Trinidadian means of co-operative saving — the sou-sou — (see p. 145) both show how close Brakes still is to his West Indian background.

The 'West End' (p. 145) refers to the fashionable part of London where all the large shops, theatres, etc. are situated. 'The Dilly' is short for Piccadilly Circus whose statue of the Greek god Eros is one of London's main landmarks. Trafalgar Square, with its famous fountains and Nelson's Column, is in easy walking distance.

Soho (p. 146) is a rather run-down, very cosmopolitan area close to Piccadilly Circus. A 'tanner' was slang for a sixpence — or half a shilling — in pre-decimal currency.

The poem Brakes has in mind on page 147 is Shelley's famous 'Ode to the West Wind' which ends 'If Winter comes, can Spring be far behind'.

The Cricket Match
This is an altogether more light-hearted story which revolves around the popular English view — or stereotype — of all West Indians as enthusiastic and talented cricketers. Algernon is quite happy to exploit this belief for his own ends although it is only almost by accident that his attempt to do so does not end disastrously.

Note: 'Nordics' (p. 149) is a word Selvon uses several times when he is referring to whites, although these whites are of course Englishmen not Norwegians!

Walcott (p. 149) was a member of the famous three W's trio of West Indian cricketers: Frank Worrell, Everton Weekes and Clyde Walcott.

Obeah in the Grove

The 'Grove' referred to here is the area of London known as Ladbroke Grove, a mainly run-down area which shows that not all the areas around the West End are 'posh'. (See 'Waiting for Aunty to Cough' where Brackley and his friends live in the same area.) This story shows how hard it was becoming to find and keep decent accommodation. This was the period when slum landlords were in their heyday and West Indians were often among their victims. The story also shows how such West Indians were adapting their West Indian customs – including, here, a belief in obeah – to their new London setting. It gives a very depressing view of relations between West Indians and their English neighbours.

Note: A 'rake' (p. 156) is a Trinidadian word for a story while 'spades' is a slang word for black people. Many of the old tenants mentioned here would have been on fixed rents of a few shillings a week while their flats could have been re-let as furnished accommodation at greatly increased rents. A 'put-you-up' is a sofa or couch which turns into a bed at night.

'Bendix' (p. 157) is another name for a laundrette where people can go to wash their dirty clothes.

Basement Lullaby

This story, with its account once more of appalling housing conditions and winter smog, gives a very depressing view of West Indian life in London. The two friends here seem to lead a totally closed in, claustrophobic life – they hardly ever even see daylight – in total contrast to the sort of lives they would have led in Trinidad. If there is any humour in this story it is of a rather bitter variety.

Note: Bar 20 probably mentions the sum of £75,000 on page 165 because this was for a time the top prize money awarded by the football pools.

The use of the word 'niggergram' on page 165 shows how Selvon's varied use of language extends not merely to reflecting what he hears but to inventing new words (see the quotation from George Lamming on page xxviii).

The reference to the smog on page 167 is to the thick fog which, until recent 'Clean Air' laws were passed, used regularly to blanket London and other major British industrial cities in winter.

'a two-and-six' (p. 168) or 'half-crown' was a common coin in pre-decimal coinage.

My Girl and the City

Although this story is set at the same time as the story 'Calypso in London' with which this section opened – i.e. the time of the Suez Crisis in 1956 (see the reference to 'Suez Deadlock' on p. 172 here) – it could hardly be more different. 'Calypso in London' had been almost entirely West Indian in language and feeling, a nearly perfect example of Selvon's calyposonian ballad style. This story, on the other hand, has almost nothing to show it is written by a West Indian; the only indication we have that the narrator seems to be a foreigner, possibly Selvon himself, is at the top of page 174 where he refers to 'the first time I ever queued in this country in '50...' (which was the year Selvon arrived in Britain). But the feeling of passionate involvement with London as a city which this story describes is perhaps all the more remarkable for being written by a foreigner who had only lived in London for a few years. And while this story is certainly a celebration of a love affair with a girl, it is at the same time a celebration of the city within and around which this love affair takes place.

There is a long passage in *The Lonely Londoners* which celebrates, in a decidedly ballad style, the glories of an English summer. In this story we have a celebration – in entirely standard and at times extremely lyrical English – of the less obvious beauties of London in all weathers and at all seasons in a way it has seldom been celebrated before. It is, as one English reviewer describes it, 'an unforgettable London Rhapsody' and illustrates once more Selvon's command of many different styles and levels of language. This story does not, however, give an over-romantic view of London; a recurrent theme which runs through the story is that of personal isolation and loneliness in the midst of crowds and in this it is close to many of Selvon's other stories and novels about life in London.

Finally 'My Girl and the City' is interesting because in it Selvon is writing *as a writer*, discussing directly the process and problems of communicating through the spoken and written word.

Note: 'There is no substitute for wool' (p. 169). This is a reference to a popular advertisement of the time which passengers could expect to see every day on the underground. Similar advertisements recur in this story, for example the one for Hall's wine on page 172 and for Amplex (a medical preparation supposed to prevent bad breath) on page 176.

A 'stenographer' (p. 172) is a shorthand writer and 'the Inner Circle' here refers to the Circle line of the underground system.

'Cleopatra's Needle' (p. 173) is a famous landmark on the Embankment. It is a large needle-shaped piece of masonry, or obelisk, brought from Egypt in the nineteenth century and named after a famous ancient Queen of Egypt.

A 'busker' (p. 174) is a street performer who entertains people in queues outside theatres, etc.

The reference to the sound the train wheels make near the bottom of page 175 is to the popular nursery rhyme 'London Bridge is falling down'.

Note on Selvon's use of language

We have noticed the great range of Selvon's use of language and he himself has always spelt out the importance of language and idiom:

> There was no other way, I tried to write *Lonely Londoners* in Standard English and it just would not work, and when I got into the Trinidad way of speaking the whole thing seemed to flow so easily and everything seemed to come to life. This idiom is so much a part of the people, so much a part of the characteristics of the people that you cannot separate a language from the experiences.[3]

George Lamming has drawn attention to the 'peasant' nature of Selvon's writing (although Selvon did not come from a peasant background himself). This is particularly marked in his use of language and one of Selvon's greatest achievements has been in helping to make the use of dialect respectable by using it not only to reproduce the language of the characters but often for the narration as well, when the author speaks as it were in his own voice. (Before *A Brighter Sun* almost the only other West Indian writer to use dialect as the language of narration had been the Jamaican writer V. S. Reid in *New Day* (1949).) The West Indian critic Kenneth Ramchand has written (in his important book *The West Indian Novel and its Background*) of Selvon's treatment of Tiger in *A Brighter Sun:* 'In following the character's inner workings in a credible modification of dialect Selvon helps to make dialect a more flexible instrument' (p. 105) and of how 'it is in this novel that dialect first becomes the language of consciousness in West Indian fiction'. Of the story 'Brackley and the Bed' in *Ways of Sunlight* he commented: 'This is as far as any West Indian author has gone towards closing the gap between the language of narration and the language of the fictional character' (p. 102).

But the word 'dialect' needs to be used with care. When Selvon started to write in the 1950s it was almost universally believed that the language which most of the people in the West Indies actually

[3] See Interview with Susheila Nasta in *Wasafiri* p.6.

spoke (rather than what they were taught in school) was merely a dialect of Standard English. However, in recent years there has been an increased awareness that what were thought to be merely inferior types of English are in fact varieties or dialects of a language – West Indian Creole – which exists in its own right with a structure and vocabulary of its own. And although West Indian Creole certainly has some affinities with Standard English it also has affinities with West African languages, with Portuguese, with Dutch, French, Spanish, and all the various other influences which have contributed to its development over the years. So perhaps it would be more accurate to talk of Selvon's use of language as an exploration of the various levels, or dialects, of language in use in the West Indies and amongst West Indian communities in London. This ranges from the pure use of Creole at one end of what is called the 'language continuum'[4] to the pure use of Standard English at the other, with many different levels in between. It is remarkable how Selvon is able to range between the different levels, adapting and modifying his language to the characters or situations he is describing. He is able to use one language, for instance, for the East Indian peasant, another for the creolised Trinidadian in the cities and yet another for the West Indian immigrant to London. It will perhaps be helpful to use the table opposite to explain this.

We must also remember that Selvon is not merely *recording* how language is used, he is also himself using language creatively and helping to invent it. George Lamming paid tribute to Selvon's inventive use of language when he described how Selvon would assign nicknames to people he knew and one of the memorable things about *Ways of Sunlight* is the vivid use of nicknames. Lamming wrote:

...Selvon is a master of this kind of invention. The contracted

[4]This is a term which linguists use to show that different dialects and levels of language overlap rather as the colours in a rainbow do, so that it is often difficult to say exactly where one starts and another ends.

Selvon's use of language in Ways of Sunlight

CREOLE	
1A *Indian Creole dialect* Used in conversation of Indian peasants	**1B** *Trinidad Creole* Used in conversation of most local characters in Trinidad stories
2 *Port of Spain Creole dialect* Used by 'hep' characters: lots of slang, Americanisms, etc. as well as basic Creole	
3 *London Creole dialect* Similar to 2 but also includes words from other West Indian Creoles and English slang	
4 *West Indian Standard* Modified narrative speech used by author. Usually nearer to Standard English than 2 or 3 but with definite West Indian flavour — although at times very close to 2 and 3	
5A *Standard English* Sometimes used in narration	**5B** *Spoken idiomatic English* Used by English characters
STANDARD ENGLISH	

phrase, niggergram, meaning the circulation of rumour at top speed, is his discovery. There can hardly be another writer who has contributed in this way to the vocabulary of West Indian conversation.[5]

Selvon himself acknowledged this when he wrote recently: 'I

[5]In *The Pleasures of Exile*, p.220.

have obviously experimented and created certain patterns of speech which are unique in themselves.' Interviewed after his arrival in Canada he said he considered his particular use of language his 'major contribution to Third World and West Indian literature'. In the process of evolving this language he had, he continued, succeeded 'in revitalising the English language by means of the Caribbean dialect'. *Ways of Sunlight* gives a good illustration of the full range and originality of Selvon's use of language.

Jane Grant 1987

Publishers' note (1994)

Sam Selvon died on April 16th, 1994, aged 70.

In addition to *Ways of Sunlight,* he published ten novels, and many essays and poems. He also received many literary awards, and two honorary doctrates from the University of Warwick, and the University of the West Indies.

Part One Trinidad

Johnson and the Cascadura

THERE'S A NATIVE legend in Trinidad which says that those who eat the cascadura will end their days in the island no matter where they wander. The cascadura is a small horny-scaled fish found in the muddy slushes of streams, and it makes a delectable dish which few tourists know about, mainly because nobody in Trinidad seems to have enough acumen to advertise it as a tourist attraction. And I suppose, too, because the city-bred inhabitants themselves might never have bothered to investigate the tastiness of the dish, only hearing of it from a friend or relative living in the country district, for even in that tiny island there is the difference of city and village with all that it entails. The flesh of the fish is as fine as that of the sardine, without the freshness, but with a taste all its own, and if you eat it curried – especially as the country natives prepare it, grinding the ingredients of the curry themselves on a flat stone – it is truly a dish worthy of remark.

Why I tell you about the legend is because it may have a bearing on the story I'm going to tell you. I say 'may' because I don't know, some people have their own beliefs and others other. For my part, I have seen and heard enough in my lifetime to keep quiet whenever there is talk of anything extraordinary or unnatural, because you can't really tell about these things. As I told Garry Johnson when we used to talk on the estate.

Johnson was an Englishman who had come out to Trinidad to spend a holiday on his friend Franklin's estate in Sangre Grande, a district some twenty-odd miles from Port of Spain, a seemingly short distance but far enough in the island to make the difference of say a village eighty miles or so from London. He had left England in winter and was eager for the sunlight, much of which we had to give him. During the day it was hot enough, but in the evening wind came from the hills and it was almost balmy, a delightful spell before night fell and made it even cooler, a time when the three of us used to sit out on the verandah of the house and sip rum punches with crushed ice.

For Franklin was a human being before anything else, and though I had my own house in the village his was open to me at all times. That I was overseer of the estate had nothing to do with it, though the villagers secretly thought I was favoured because of my position. Franklin was middle-aged, with greying hair. Before he bought the cocoa estate it was going to ruin. The price of cocoa had fallen in the world market, and the previous owner put the estate up for sale. It was advertised in the English newspapers – 'rich cocoa plantation in the West Indies for sale, owner retiring' – and Franklin got to hear of it. At the time he was considering emigrating from England and it looked like a good proposition to him. He was single, he had no ties, and a country away from the rigours of the English climate was just what he wanted.

In fact, he and Johnson had planned to come out to the island together, but at the last moment Johnson changed his mind.

Franklin treated his labourers well and the estate thrived. Even in the village he was respected for his kindness. When the dry season lingered on, the villagers would come for water from the two huge concrete cisterns on the estate, carrying it away in barrels on donkey carts. He could have made them pay and they would have thought it only fair: they offered him money from the little they earned toiling in the canefields and in their gardens, but Franklin always shook his head and told them they could have anything they wanted on the plantation. So it was that he became godfather for many a ragged little child in the village, and no ceremony was held without an invitation to him.

My duties as overseer were to keep the estate working smoothly, and get the cocoa ready for market. Those evenings drinking rum punches on the verandah was a usual thing with us before Johnson came, for it was a chance to talk of the estate, what should be done about the last trees we planted, or if we needed more immortelles to shade the young trees on the plantation, and shop like that.

Johnson was a lot younger than Franklin. He was vigorous and active. He got up early in the morning and breathed great gulps of air long before either Franklin or myself was out of bed. He used to watch the girls who came from the village to 'dance' the cocoa seeds where they dried in the sun. The seeds were scattered on a large platform over which was a roof of galvanised sheets. The roof rested on wheels on the platform, so that it could be quickly rolled away – away when the sun was shining, back over the platform at the least sign of rain, for a downpour on the drying seeds would ruin all our labour. The girls 'danced' among the cocoa, turning them to and fro with their bare feet to ensure even curing. And Johnson sometimes joined them, and the girls would blush and titter to see the white man with his trousers rolled up, imitating the movements they made.

He spent most of the day roaming the plantation with me, anxious to learn all about the estate, for he had money invested in it, though he confessed to me that he had no real interest in this sort of life, and had only come to the island because he hoped to get background material for a book he was writing, on superstition and witchcraft.

'You'll get a lot of information here,' I told him, 'the villagers are very superstitious.'

But it was in the evenings that we really waxed warm on the subject. Although I myself held a neutral opinion about such things, I told Johnson such tales of local superstition as I knew. About Papa Bois, a spirit who lurked in the forests and lured evil hunters away from beaten tracks so that they were lost for days in the jungle. He heard of soucouyants which sucked your blood while you slept, and of balls of fire which appeared from nowhere and scared the people in lonely spots in the night. You could only escape from *la diablesse* by shooting it with a silver bullet, I explained, or if you see it approaching, quickly draw the sign of the cross in the air in front of you, and that will keep the evil spirit away.

All this Johnson used to put down in a little notebook he kept. Franklin for his part listened more than talked, but he did say how one night he was coming in late from inspecting some young orange trees at the other end of the plantation, and a flaming ball of fire shot across the path and his horse got wild and galloped away, or else he didn't know what he would have done.

'What do you mean, a flaming ball of fire?' Johnson asked, hoping to get some reasoning from Franklin.

But Franklin only shrugged and pulled at his pipe. 'That is what it was,' he said. 'I can't explain it any other way. I went back the next day, because I remembered the exact spot, but there was nothing to see.'

'Come now,' Johnson said, 'you don't believe all this rigmarole that Sam has been telling us?'

Franklin sloshed the ice in his glass of punch. 'I've been out here longer than you have.' And he wouldn't say more than that.

Sometimes we sent for a labourer to get a first-hand account of some weird experience. Once Chanko, the old Indian watchman, came and told us how one night he heard a rattle of chains as if dragged by some powerful animal, but he couldn't see a thing.

'All-you wouldn't believe me, chief, but it had a man in the village name Santogee, who used to work obeah and turn animal in the night, and go all about the village frightening people. So when we find out is he who doing all this business, we make up a head and decide to chase him out, and since he gone all the noise and thing in the night did stop.'

'Did you ever see a soucouyant?' Johnson asked him, busily writing in his notebook.

'Oh God Mr Johnson, don't call that thing name! If I ever see one! It had a time down Icacos, when I was walking in the coconut one night, and the wind did blowing strong, and what I could see but this piece of light, like fire in the air, coming at me. So I run out on the beach for my life, as I thought it wouldn't follow me there. But I see the thing still coming. I was so frighten! But I stop and take my cutlass and I make the sign of the cross in the sand. I bawl out, "Come now, let we see who is man!" And you know what happen? The light come right up to that cross and it couldn't pass it. It make two-three circle in the air, trying to pass by the side of the cross, but everytime it do that I make another cross, and in the end I had a circle of cross all round me, and I in the centre, and this thing going round and round in the air, until suddenly it disappear. Is really true, Mr Johnson, bad things does run from the sign of the cross.'

'This thing was quite near to you?' Johnson asked.

'About from where you sitting to where I standing,' Chanko said.

'What did it look like?'

'Look like? I didn't look too close Mr Johnson, but it look like a ball of fire.'

Chanko would need a drink to wet his throat for him to continue, and as the labourers favoured rum more than whisky Franklin usually had a bottle of local rum to hand. Once he was under way there was no stopping Chanko, and I know that he made up a lot to tell the Englishmen as he went on, but no harm was done and I never said anything.

Whenever Johnson was not on the estate we took it that he

was out collecting material for his book. He had made a few friends in the village and the natives were pleased to help him when they learnt that he was going to write a book about them, as they thought.

And then a rumour began to drift around. It started as a feeling in the atmosphere. You can't pin a rumour down, or exactly explain how it gets into motion, but once started it takes a lot to stop it. First I noticed the girls who were dancing the cocoa whispering and smiling among themselves, as if at a secret joke. Then I heard them talking, and Johnson's name was mentioned.

'What's that about Mr Johnson?' I asked Seeta, a young Indian girl who should really have been attending school, but whose parents were so poor that she had to begin work at an early age.

'Nothing boss,' she said quickly. They all called me 'boss'.

'What is it?' I said sternly.

The girl hung her head. 'We was just talking about Mr Johnson and Urmilla.'

She would say nothing more than that, though I threatened her job, and I let her go ahead with her work and wandered off into the cocoa under the pretext that I wanted to have a look at a set of young plants we were experimenting with in a valley near the hills. I knew that I wanted a chance to think things out.

Urmilla was the most beautiful Indian girl I had ever seen. It was a withdrawn sort of beauty, you only saw it when she was disturbed, like the time when her father wanted to marry her off to a rich merchant in the city. How Urmilla defied her father's wishes I never found out, but she didn't marry the merchant after all, despite the custom of her people of arranging marriages for their children and strictly controlling their lives up to that point, and sometimes even after that. And in those weeks when the marriage was in the air she bore herself with a kind of comely defiance, and the beauty that was withdrawn came to the surface, and her face was rosy and her eyes bright as pearls, and she had a way sometimes of tossing her long hair, as if in her mind she was having words with her father. Sookdeo, aware of his daughter's fascination, had been anxious to have her married and shift the responsibility from his shoulders. He took the problem to Franklin, but the Englishman was too wise to offer advice one way or the other in a family matter like that. He listened patiently to Sookdeo, and when he was finished he said there was nothing that he could do. However, if Sookdeo wanted, the girl could work on the estate – there were many odd jobs around. Sookdeo took that as being Franklin's decision on the whole matter, and the next day he sent Urmilla to work.

The girl worked well, and always managed to turn the advances of the men on the estate into a joke, and make the most serious approach seem as playful fun, and after a time the men let her alone, though there was not one – and I include myself – who would not have married her at the snap of a finger.

Johnson had remarked on the girl's beauty one morning as she danced the cocoa, and later on I saw him talking to her. He walked to the village with her that evening when her work was finished. After that, I saw them sometimes together. That is to say, she would be working and Johnson would be helping her – he often did this with the women on the estate. Or else they would be walking away to whatever part of the estate Urmilla's work called her.

And that was all, until the rumour began to spread.

Now I am not one of those persons who stick their heads in the sand and pretend not to notice things, or scoff when suspicion is in the air. After all, Johnson was a young man, and Urmilla was just at the age of merging into graceful womanhood. That he was a white man and she an Indian did not make any difference at this stage. For companionship of his own society he would have to travel into the capital – a thing which Franklin himself used to do in the beginning, until he really settled down on the estate. And then he wouldn't budge except he had to go on business. On rare occasions – on Sundays, if at all – he had visitors from the city. When Johnson came he did speak about this, and offered to drive him into Port of Spain whenever he felt like it, or use the car himself if he wanted. But Johnson, too, seemed satisfied rambling around the district, and I never saw him using the car.

What was wrong if he was seen in Urmilla's company? Nothing, I told myself. Nothing, and yet . . . I shrugged as I thought. In a way, it was none of my business. If Franklin didn't know or say anything, then I would hold my tongue. In any case, what could I say? Certainly nothing to Johnson. True we were friends, but I wouldn't know how to approach him with a personal thing like that. And Urmilla? She would probably laugh and tell me that I was jealous. But it wasn't jealousy that made me think that way. I was an Indian myself, and I knew that if their relationship came to light – if there was in fact, such a relationship, for so far there was nothing but the rumour – there would be hell to pay. White people feel they are stepping down when they fraternise with coloured people: they don't always seem to realise that it is just as shameful if not more so for the other party. Not that Johnson was a snob or anything like that, but I knew that old Sookdeo would kick up hell if he suspected anything. He had allowed Urmilla to come to the estate because he believed that Franklin would keep an eye on her – a responsibility which Franklin had never admitted, but which the Indian took for granted.

That evening I deliberately sought Franklin when he was alone, and tried to see if I could get anything out of him. But if he knew about the rumour at all he kept his mouth shut. Not a word or any remark to give me a clue. As for Johnson himself, there was nothing he said or did to indicate when he joined us later for our usual evening siesta on the veranda, that he was disturbed in any way, and I decided to leave things as they were until something happened.

But next morning Urmilla herself started the suspicion again in my mind. She was mending some cocoa bags – sewing the holes with twine – in a corner of the shed in which we stored the empty pods. I had entered the shed searching for a cutlass which I had misplaced. As soon as she saw me Urmilla said,

'Sam, when Mr Johnson going back England?'

'Why do you want to know?' I asked.

Urmilla kept her head bent over her work. 'Oh, I was only wondering.'

'Mr Johnson is Mr Franklin's guest,' I said coldly, unable to resist getting back at her for rejecting my advances in the past. 'It is none of your business.'

But that flared Urmilla and brought the beauty to her face. She looked up and where her eyes should have been I saw pearls. 'He tell me himself when he is going,' she cried, 'I don't have to find out from you!'

This was perhaps the time to find out if there was anything going on between them, but I held myself back. After all, what concern was it of mine? It was up to Franklin to put a stop to the matter.

I muttered something under my breath to save face and left her.

That afternoon was the hottest I ever knew. One takes the constant sun for granted, living in the island, and the heat is never a topic of conversation. Clouds are always drifting across the sun and offering a few minutes of relief. But the sky now was so clear that a white heat seemed spread over the blue, and the sun had lost its dazzle, as if it had settled down to the job of setting the earth on fire, and it burned steadfast and strong. Leaves drooped in the heavy, motionless atmosphere and a kind of sleepy hush fell on the estate. Not a bird twittered in the trees – dogs, cats, poultry, all had left the open spaces and sought shade. I couldn't see a labourer in sight, and it would have been heartless to seek them out from wherever they were and order them to go on working.

I thought it a good idea to take a stroll by the river, part of which ran through the plantation, and plunge into the water for a few minutes.

I had just emerged from a clump of bushes when I saw them on the opposite bank. I drew back quickly.

It was Urmilla and Johnson.

They were sitting on the grass, she had a long shoot of grass in her hand and she was moving it against his cheek.

The old longing I had thought dead rose in me like a flame. There was no mistaking their attitude. It was one of love. I was so jealous I bit my lip until it bled.

And then they kissed. I stood looking, a sort of numb pain running all over my body, my throat so dry I couldn't swallow. I stood a long time and still his lips were on hers. It was very still, nothing moved.

And then I could look no more. I stumbled my way back, not caring if they heard me, and my mind was numb with an aching pain.

As soon as I got back to the yard a labourer said, 'Boss, Mr Franklin look for you.'

'Where is he?' I said.

'Up at the house, in the office, boss.'

When I got there I knew what it was about. He was always outspoken with me, and came to the point without hedging, but this time he was obviously uneasy and didn't know how to begin.

'Sit down – have a drink,' he said, waving his hand at a bottle of Scotch.

I did both, spooning ice from a jug into my glass and adding a touch of lime juice, before I took a seat.

It was very quiet. There were no sounds of work near the house. Poultry were scratching in the yard. From where I sat I could look out the window and see the huts of the village in the distance.

'Do you know where Johnson is?'

Urmilla was the only one who said 'Garry'. I had taken my cue from Franklin ever since he came, and I never bothered to ask why.

'I suppose he's in the village or knocking about the plantation,' I said.

Then he said, 'You know Sookdeo's daughter, don't you?'

I didn't bother to answer that, because Franklin knew. I just waited, shutting my mind from the picture on the bank of the river.

'There've been rumours going around.' Franklin got up and stood near the window, blocking my view of the village. 'Have you heard anything?'

'Like what?' I asked innocently.

Franklin got angry at that. 'You know more than I do,' he said, turning from the window. 'You're among the labourers all the time, you must have heard what they're saying. Don't pretend with me, Sam.'

'If you mean about Johnson and Urmilla,' I said, 'I don't know more than you do. The labourers are talking, all right, but that doesn't prove a thing. You know how they are. To see a white man going about like that with a native girl must have made them curious and talkative.'

'I don't like it,' Franklin said. 'I don't like it at all. How long have these rumours been going on? Why haven't you told me about it before?'

He didn't wait for an answer to that. He poured himself a drink and went on, 'Listen, Sam you're an Indian yourself, but somehow you're different. You know what this can do. You've got to stop it. It's up to you. Let the girl leave the estate, if you have to.'

'That wouldn't do any good,' I said. 'If they want to see each other they'll find a way. Why don't you drop a hint to Johnson?' I had worked with Franklin a long time and I wasn't afraid to suggest that to him.

But he shook his head. 'I don't think there's anything in it myself,' he said, 'but the gossip could cause trouble. There's no need to let on to Johnson that we know anything. But you do what you can to stop the labourers from talking, Sam. Johnson's only here for three weeks more, anyway, and I don't want to spoil it for him, he seems to be enjoying his holiday.' Then he changed the subject. 'I'm going to town and may be back late.'

All well and good for Franklin to say kill the rumour, I thought, as I left the office, but what was I supposed to do? Call the labourers together and make a speech to them? Tell them they weren't to talk about Mr Johnson and Urmilla?

Late in the afternoon I noticed that Urmilla was not around. There was nothing unusual in this, she could be anywhere on the estate, but somehow I felt uneasy. I didn't see Johnson around, either.

The labourers had finished work and gone home, and I was banding a cutlass handle with wire, sitting on what we used to call a 'copper' – a huge metal basin, found on estates in the country districts and presumably used at one time for storing water; this one was rusty and upside-down – when I saw Urmilla hurrying from a wooded part of the plantation. When she got up to me she was exhausted and could hardly speak. Her hair was wild and her face rosy, and her breasts heaved with heavy breathing.

'What's the matter?' I cried, jumping off the 'copper'.

'It's Garry,' she gasped, leaning on my arm, 'he climb a tree and now he can't come down.'

'Where is the tree?' I asked, more amused than alarmed.

'Come, I show you,' and exhausted as she was Urmilla turned and began to walk swiftly back into the plantation.

It was only as we were hurrying to the spot that I realised she had called Johnson by his first name.

Johnson had climbed an immortelle tree. How he managed I don't know, for the trunk of this tree is so stout it sometimes takes three men with outstretched arms to encircle it, and no branches grow for about twelve to eighteen feet off the ground. The trunk was rough, but even so it didn't offer much of a foothold. I had never heard of anyone climbing an immortelle – in the first place, why? The tree was planted on the estate to shade the growing cocoa from the sun, and it bore a beautiful blossom, but no fruit.

Why should anyone want to climb an immortelle?

Johnson sang out when he saw us, 'Hello there'. He was sitting in the first fork – quite eighteen feet from the ground – with his feet wrapped around the branch. He was smoking.

'What are you doing up there?' I couldn't help the question.

'Tell you later,' Johnson said calmly. 'But get me off first. My hands and knees are bruised with the climbing, and I don't want to risk further damage coming down. Can you get a rope or something?'

There was a ladder at the house, but it wasn't long enough. As for rope – I cast my eyes about, looking for a vine – 'supple-jack' we called the variety on the estate. I found one a short distance away and cut it. I flung one end up to Johnson, and he wrapped it around the branch and twisted it again and again, tucking in the end.

'Let me try it first,' I said, and I tugged with all my strength. It held.

Johnson came down cautiously, holding on to the vine with both hands, and sliding down the trunk with his feet. He had to drop the last six feet, holding the vine, but his height made this easy. He stumbled when he fell and got up quickly.

All this time Urmilla had been silently watching on. Once Johnson was safe on the ground she turned to go. It seemed as if he wanted to say something to her, but he checked himself.

Franklin and I got the story out of him that evening as we sat drinking. The day had been hot, but now the wind was cool and scented with guava blossoms, and there was a twilight atmosphere on the estate. This was the time of year for such light – a brief three weeks when the day hesitated before plunging into night: for the rest of the year, from the moment the sun sank it began to get dark, and in a few minutes night descended.

Johnson had been told by a native that the egg of a corbeau – local name for a vulture – was a lucky charm, that the possessor only had to ask for what he wanted, and Aladdin-lamp-like, it was his. But if he took an egg, he had to replace it with an ordinary domestic one, hard-boiled. So he had set off to look for a corbeau's nest, and thought he saw one in the immortelle tree. After his struggle to climb he found it was only a broken branch with dry leaves.

'Corbeaux don't nest in trees,' I told him, after we had laughed so much that Franklin spilt his drink, 'you find them in holes in the ground, near bushy places, or in the trunks of dead trees.'

'Ever heard that one before – about the lucky charm, I mean?' Johnson asked Franklin.

Franklin shook his head sleepily. He had only returned from Port of Spain a short while and he looked tired. After another drink he left us and went to bed.

'I thought it was something serious, the way Urmilla came racing out of the plantation,' I said. This was the first time I had ever mentioned the girl's name to him.

'Yes,' Johnson said slowly, as if he were thinking of something. 'This girl, Urmilla, what do you know about her, Sam?'

'There isn't much to know about poor people in a small village,' I said, but I told him how once her father wanted her to marry and she wouldn't have it.

Johnson got up and sat on the wooden top of the railing at the edge of the veranda, and he looked up at the hills.

'I love her, Sam,' he said.

I didn't know what to say: what could I say? Sometimes people tell you things and then expect you to comment as if it were your duty to do so, and you don't really know what to tell them. I didn't know if Johnson expected me to say something, but I kept quiet, not that I had any choice. I was thinking about the time when I was in love with Urmilla myself, a love which would still have existed if she didn't kill it slowly with a kind of day to day indifference until I knew it was no use, she didn't and wouldn't love me no matter what I did. No matter how strong love is it could die that way, with no reciprocation whatsoever. What had hurt me most was that she was always friendly to me, there was no question of dislike or hatred. I hated her when she first told me, but I had learnt to bear my pain quietly. Now, she didn't matter so much to me again. I intended to work some more years on the plantation and save my money – there was no place around to spend it, anyway – and then go to America. That was my goal, and ever since the decision I had kept it in front of me like an image to bar the memory of her, and it wasn't difficult anymore to think of my future. And seeing her every day on the estate had made me accustomed to the sight of her, though there was still a catch in my throat sometimes which no one ever knew about. I had a funny feeling when Johnson said, 'I love her, Sam.' I didn't expect him to say that, nor the way he said it. It made me realise my own true feelings for Urmilla. It had been all right to bear the rejection while I knew there was no one she was likely to fall in love with. Now that this had happened, I felt that silly catch in my throat once more. I tried hard to think of America, of my ambition to save and go away to another country.

'But you're going back to England in a couple of weeks,' I said. I had wanted to say that to myself, as a sort of consolation, but the words came out.

'I know,' he said.

After that he was silent, and he didn't even know when I left, he was staring out to the hills, where darkness was making weird shapes of trees and risings.

The next day Sookdeo came to see Franklin. We were in

the office, checking some accounts which Franklin had brought back from his trip to the city, when a labourer stood outside the window – it was quite low, and pushed open on a stick – and called out that Sookdeo wanted to see Mr Franklin.

Franklin looked at me, and I looked at him. I hadn't slept well that night. My eyes were red and I had a pain in the back of my head. I rose to go.

'You might as well stay and hear what he has to say,' Franklin said, motioning me to sit down again.

Sookdeo came in and stood holding an old felt hat in his hand, turning it round and round. It must have needed a lot of courage to come to Franklin.

'Mr Franklin,' Sookdeo said, 'we having a christening in the village tomorrow for Doolsie child, and we want you to stand godfather, please.'

Franklin breathed a sigh of relief. I admitted to myself that I was disappointed.

'Certainly, Sookdeo. What time is it?'

'In the evening time, when sun set.' Sookdeo still turned the hat, like how the women turn a *roti* round before slapping it on the baking iron.

'Have a drink,' Franklin offered, as the Indian still stood there uneasily.

Sookdeo looked at the bottle of Scotch and gulped. I poured a drink and handed it to him. He swallowed it neatly, quickly, and returned the glass.

'Thanks Mr Franklin,' he said, wiping his sleeve across his mouth.

He turned as if to go. Halfway to the door he stopped and turned again. The drink had given him the courage he needed to talk.

'Mr Franklin,' he blurted out, 'when I send Urmilla here I thought you going take care of she and keep she out of trouble.' He hesitated, then went on, 'Now I hearing things about she and Mr Johnson that I don't like at all. Mr Johnson is a white man, and I respect him, but he must respect we Indians too. Urmilla not for him, and I want you to tell him to leave the girl alone, Mr Franklin, or else trouble start on the estate and in the village.'

'What things have you been hearing, Sookdeo?' Franklin asked.

The Indian waved his hand in the air vaguely. 'All sorts of things, about how Mr Johnson always seen with the girl, in the village, and on the estate, and all about. Ramdeen tell me one day he see she with he hand round she waist, and another time he see them down by the river together.'

'I never knew you listened to the gossip of other people, Sookdeo,' Franklin said reprovingly. But I knew that he felt there was truth in all this, and he was only fencing around for a way to make the matter pass off as decently as possible.

He turned to me and said, 'You're on the estate all the time, Sam. Have you ever seen Mr Johnson with Sookdeo's daughter?'

I thought of the time I had seen them on the bank of the river, and of the kiss that for me was never ended. I still saw them in my dreams. He was holding her, and she clung to him as how a vine clings to a tree, as if she were wrapped around him, and I saw his lips coming down on hers. And the dream used to stay like that, with them kissing that one kiss, on and on, as if they were frozen and would never let loose of each other.

'No,' I lied. What was I, big-heart or something? Why didn't I put Sookdeo on the warpath before it was too late?

'I see for myself,' Sookdeo said, and now his voice was no longer respectful. 'One evening I passing in the track near to the hill behind the plantation, and I hear voices in the bush. When I look, what you think I see? I see Urmilla laying down in the grass with Mr Johnson, and they was doing all kinds of things that I don't have to tell you ...'

I rose to go, to get away from all this, my heart thumping in my chest.

But when I got outside Sookdeo's voice followed me and

stayed with me. I got my cutlass and I went into the plantation where the labourers were clearing a piece of land, and I hacked with them at the bush and shrub and knotty grass, and Sookdeo said, ' . . . they was doing all kinds of things that I don't have to tell you . . . '

I skipped the get-together for a drink that evening. Nobody knew how it was with me concerning Urmilla, and I was afraid I might say or do something emotional and give myself away. The village offering no entertainment, I had been happy to spend the evenings with the two Englishmen. I didn't know what to do with myself. I tried to read some magazines, and I tried not to hate the Englishmen. I had always boasted to myself a broad mind and a wide philosophy which embraced the whole world. Now I was thinking in terms of colour, of black and white. What right had Johnson to come across thousands of miles of ocean from England and turn the course of my life like that? Was he going to marry Urmilla and take her away to England? The girl was a fool to believe anything he said. You never could trust these white people who came out from England, they laughed and talked with you but when it came to a serious matter they always felt themselves superior . . .

I suddenly realised how foolish I was and I laughed aloud. Love could do that to a man, I thought, it could make him lose his reason.

I was irritable with myself. I lit a cigarette and after I had taken a few puffs I decided to go back to the estate. I could always tell Franklin that I had had something to attend to in the village, and had to leave early.

When I got there the pattern was as usual: Franklin in his rocking chair and slippers, Johnson in an easy chair slumped so low I only saw his hand moving as he sloshed the ice in his glass of punch.

I intended to act as if nothing had happened, and had in fact a sentence already framed in my mind to ask Johnson how his book was getting on.. But they had been talking about Urmilla. I knew from the way they stopped as soon as I appeared, and it threw me off the balance, as it were, and I only said hello, and took a long time pouring myself a drink.

'I have just been telling Johnson that Sookdeo came to see me today,' Franklin said.

'Oh,' I said, trying to pretend I wasn't particularly interested.

'Johnson says he is sorry for having started this, and that he won't see the girl anymore, before he leaves next week.'

'Next week?' I asked.

'Yes,' Johnson's voice came from the depths of the easy chair. 'There's a ship leaving and I know one of the officers on board. That will brighten the long voyage.'

'Oh,' I said again.

Then Franklin himself changed the subject, and we got around to superstitions and black magic and that sort of thing, but Franklin and myself did most of the talking.

When I was leaving Johnson said he wanted a bit of fresh air and would walk halfway to the village with me.

Stars covered the sky in such profusion it was almost as if there was moonlight. The night was cool, with a gentle breeze bringing the scent of wild bush.

I hoped with all my heart that Johnson wasn't going to pour out his feelings to me. But it was a hope in vain. He began as soon as we were clear of the house.

'I can't take her back to England with me,' he said.

'Of course not,' I said, as if it was the most natural thing in the world. But I was thinking, You'll break her heart.

'She knows that,' he said. 'And she understands and accepts it. She's a wonderful girl, Sam.'

'I know,' I said.

'If things were different, if I could have stayed here . . .' he sighed.

I was thinking, if I loved somebody nothing in the world would stop us from being together.

But you can't think for everybody. I couldn't think for Johnson, I didn't know anything of his background in England, or what reasons he had for what he did. Sometimes the way you think, you feel everybody else should think that way too. But it doesn't work out that way at all.

I was pleased to find myself in a rational frame of mind once more. Pleased, but I was far from happy.

Only a few days remained now before Johnson left us. We had a deadline for getting the cocoa to market, and I was fairly busy. I deliberately kept out of Urmilla's way, and if I saw her at all it was in the distance.

Franklin was giving a dinner and dance for Johnson the night before he sailed. He expected quite a few people from Port of Spain, and was even paying an orchestra to come and play for the night. One of the buildings in which the cocoa was stored was cleared out and cleaned to be used as a ballroom. The estate had never seen such activity and excitement, and it was the topic in the village from the time the news got around.

Johnson had inevitably heard the legend about the cascadura in his search for material for the book and he was determined to go fishing before he left. So that day I went out with him to a branch of the river that flowed down from the hills behind the village, with the strangest fishing gear he had ever seen.

'Don't tell me you're going fishing with a bucket and a basket,' he said.

'Wait and see,' I laughed.

There are two ways to catch the cascadura. One is to dam the muddy area where you suspect they are, and bail out the water and pick them up floundering in the mud. The other is to look for a spot where twigs and leaves and other odd debris float down and form an island near a calm part of the stream. Under such shelter the cascadura lays its eggs. All you have to do is to dip your bucket partly into the water, so that you cover the nest, and splash the water near the basket. When the fish hears the noise it leaps towards it, and you catch him in your basket and drain off the water, and you've landed your first cascadura.

I think Johnson enjoyed this excursion more than any other during his stay in the island. We had on leggings and we waded into the muddy sloshes looking for islands of leaves and dead branches at the side of the stream, and Johnson got a cascadura at his first attempt.

It was the breeding season and the only reason that we didn't come back with the basket full of cascaduras was because neither of us was expert at this sort of fishing. As it was, we got a full two dozen and we strung them on a strip of black-sage bark and walked back with them dangling in our hands.

We gave most of them away as we walked back to the estate, for Johnson took one look at them and shook his head.

'I'm not going to eat that,' he said, screwing up his face.

'They're delicious,' I said.

'I only wanted to have a look,' Johnson said.

So we gave away the last six to Sookdeo, whom we met in the village. The old man was glad for them. He went so far as to shake Johnson's hand and wish him a speedy voyage, all animosity gone now that the Englishman's departure was imminent.

I put on my best suit that evening to go to the house. I am not one for parties and dancing and that sort of thing, and Franklin knew it. Besides, the white people in Port of Spain were a snobbish lot and I don't think many of his friends would have relished the idea of the Indian overseer dancing with their wives. But Franklin had asked me to come anyway, to keep an eye on the serving and to see that everything went all right.

There was dinner and dancing as the guests felt inclined, and things went off well enough, with some dancing and others eating. Curious villagers had come and were standing on tiptoe outside the windows to have a look at the unusual grandeur in the cocoa house.

I was having a drink with myself for company when I saw someone gesturing near the door. It was Urmilla. She wore her sari like a sort of veil, hiding her face.

'What do you want?' I asked her.

'I bring something for Garry, Sam. Something for him to eat before he go. I cook it myself.'

'You can't see him now, Urmilla,' I said. 'He's dancing. With a white girl,' I added spitefully.

'All I want you to do is to give him this, and say that I cook it especially for him.' She had a ware bowl wrapped in a white towel in her hand.

'What is it?'

'Curry cascasdoo,' she said, using the local name for the fish.

I mocked her. ' "Those who eat the cascadura will, the native legend says, wheresoever they may wander end in Trinidad their days." '

Her eyes flashed but she bit her lip and held back whatever she was going to say.

'Do it for me, Sam,' she pleaded, 'just give him and say that I make it for him to eat.'

'You don't believe that legend, do you Urmilla? You don't think eating that fish is going to make Garry come back? Besides, he doesn't want to eat cascadura. We gave away all we caught today.'

'You – just – give – him – this,' she said slowly, 'and say that I make it especially for him. You will do a little favour for me, Sam?'

'All·right, all right,' I said angrily, and I took the bundle from her and put it on a table.

I not only had to bear the pain of hearing Johnson talk of his love for her, but now I had to suffer the indignity of aiding her in her love for him.

I downed another drink, then another. When I saw Johnson alone I told him.

'Where is it?' he asked.

I led him to the small room where the food was being kept. 'Is she gone?' he asked.

I nodded.

He took the towel off and looked at the dish.

'Um, it doesn't look so bad when it's cooked, does it?'

'I told you, it's delicious,' I said, without enthusiasm.

Johnson tasted it with a fork. Then he sat down and ate the lot.

Afterwards I was busy trying to get drunk by mixing every kind of drink I could lay my hands on. It must have been two hours or so later. Johnson came to me and said, 'Listen, Sam. This party is getting high. There is a suggestion of dancing and wining until the morning, and then all of us going in to Port of Spain together to see me off. I don't mind, but I've got to get away for a while.'

'What you mean,' I said drunkenly, 'is that you've got to bid a last fond farewell to your love.'

'You're getting drunk, Sam. But that is exactly what I want to do. Can't you get some girls from the village to do some Indian dancing and singing for a half hour or so to cover up my absence?'

'Sure, sure,' I said, 'bring on the dancing girls. You leave everything to me, Garry. You leave everything to me.'

And so to the last hours of his departure I was being in-volved. After the cascadura, now this. He was going off some-where to meet her, a rendezvous somewhere on the estate, under trees in the moonlight, on the soft, dewy grass . . . I started to sing a soppy sentimental song, and went off to ask the watching villagers outside if they cared to dance and sing for the white people. Two of them ran back to the village to find costumes and their own musical instruments.

I passed out drunk as a lord after that.

Time went by slowly in the valley after Johnson's de-parture, but gradually its passage increased as memory of the

Englishman dimmed, and two years went by without much
incident on the estate.

During this time I had renewed my wooing of Urmilla, but
with little success. The beauty she radiated while he was here
was withdrawn, nothing seemed to excite or interest her.

Whenever I went down to the village to collect the estate
mail she wanted to know if there was a letter from Garry for
Mr Franklin, and when he was coming back to Trinidad.

'He isn't coming back, Urmilla,' I told her again. 'He told
us that before he went away.'

'Mr Franklin must tell you what Garry write in the letters,
Sam. What he say, eh? He getting married to white girl in
England?'

Once I was in such a vicious mood with her pestering for
news about him that I said, 'He's getting married next month
to a girl who works in the office where he is.'

'You's a liar, Sam!' She said it so passionately that I hastened
to say it was untrue.

'If you want the both of we to remain friend, Sam, you
must never tell me any lie about Garry.'

'Why can't you forget him, Urmilla? Do you think he
remembers you? Now he is among his own society, do you
think he will ever come back?'

'He eat cascadoo, he must come back, even if it is to dead.'

'You can't go on living and hoping on the strength of a
thing like that,' I said earnestly. 'Even if it can't be me, then
I would rather you loved somebody else and spent the rest of
your life happily than go on like this.'

'You know anybody who ever eat cascadoo and leave Trinidad and didn't come back?'

There was no reasoning with her. Sometimes a person gets
beyond reason, and you wonder what it is they have that
sustains them, that makes them quietly strong. Urmilla was
locking her life away, as it were, awaiting his return with an
infinite patience.

Yet womanhood crept up on her, as if it were forcing a beauty on her she didn't want to accept just yet. There was nothing girlish about her now. She was ripe, and she was waiting to be plucked.

Another year went by, a year in which I tried desperately to win her love. Except for when we talked about Garry, she appeared to be a little less unhappy, and even laughed sometimes.

I knew that Sookdeo was after her to marry me, but he knew better than to try and force a marriage again. And I wouldn't have him do it.

'Leave her alone,' I told him. 'Let her make up her mind for herself.'

'She have to be married soon,' Sookdeo said. 'I getting old and sickly, and I want she to married before I dead.'

It was her father's health which finally made Urmilla decide. He fell seriously ill and was ebbing away helplessly, but before he died he made her promise to marry me.

I told her afterwards that it was all right, that I wouldn't want to hold her to the promise unless she really wanted me, but she said she was ready any time I was.

I don't know what made me delay the marriage, maybe it was some stubborn pride, but while I was giving her time to grow to love me, a letter came from Garry.

I waited to hear what the news was, and Franklin told me as soon as he read the letter.

'Johnson is ill,' he said. 'He's got a rare blood disease.'

'Is it bad?' I asked.

'They don't give him much time to live,' he said. 'He wants to come out here next month. His doctor feels he should get away from the English climate.'

I didn't want to tell Urmilla, not just yet, but she knew a letter had come that morning, and she questioned me with her eyes without saying a word.

'Johnson is coming back next month,' I said, trying hard

to make it sound casual. I didn't tell her about his illness.

I knew then that my case was utterly hopeless. I could never bring the pearls to her eyes like the news about Garry. She didn't even try to hide the joy she felt.

'Remember what I told you the night your father died, Urmilla,' I said. 'I don't hold you to any promise.'

It was funny the way everything was turning out for me.

'One thing,' I told her later, 'you must never tell Garry about us. That's a promise I would ask you to keep.'

She promised eagerly. I never stood a chance, even if I had married her.

Before Johnson arrived I made my plans. I had never completely forgotten my desire to leave the island: perhaps it was a sort of escape I kept open all the time. I had saved enough money to see me well on the way.

I told Franklin I was leaving. He knew it had to come some time, and I told him when Johnson came he would be able to help a little until he found somebody to take my place. He saw reason in this. He thanked me for all I had done – not only with words, but with money. He gave me three hundred dollars with my next wage packet.

I refused to entertain the one last hope that perhaps Johnson had forgotten all about Urmilla. I didn't bank anything on it, I was going to leave in any case. The trend of events pointed that way for me.

But Johnson hadn't forgotten, as was so obvious when they met.

He had written the book and it had been accepted for publication and he intended to go on writing. There was nothing physically wrong with him, there was just this disease that was mysteriously shortening his life.

When I left the estate, his marriage to Urmilla was already being planned. He was going to marry her according to Indian rites, and they were to settle on the estate in a house Franklin was going to build for them.

The last time I saw him, he gave me the last twist of the knife. He 'said, 'What I can't understand, Sam, is why you didn't marry Urmilla yourself. Haven't you got an eye for beauty, man?'

'My ambition was always to go abroad,' I said naïvely. 'I never thought about it.' Then I said, 'So the cascadura legend really worked, and brought you back to Trinidad.'

'I can't get Urmilla to believe otherwise,' he laughed.

Urmilla was positive that the cascadura had worked a charm. The last thing she was doing when I left the island was consulting the local obeah-man for a medicine to cure Garry's illness.

Down the Main

WHEN THE WAR did over in Trinidad in nineteen-forty-five, it had a lot of fellars who leave the forces with plenty money that they get demobilised with. Frederick for one never see so much money at one time and he start to get on ignorant and spending free-sheet. By the time he begin to take stock he see that he only have a few dollars remaining from the three hundred that the government people demobilise him with.

Round this time it had bags of fellars who was going to Venezuela to look for work. Things was rosy over there, fellars only writing home and talking about how money flowing in the country, and saying how Americans opening up the place and it have plenty work all about.

Well in truth, Venezuela is a rich country that have plenty iron and ore, and when war was finish people from all over the world was starting to go there, and it look like history repeat itself how they invading the Spanish Main looking for money.

Things would have been all right for the boys if the Venezuelan government didn't decide to get hard. They say that only a certain amount of West Indians was to be allowed to work in the country, and by the time Frederick start to hustle it had more West Indians in the country than the law allow.

But fellars wasn't worrying about that, because it had a big racket going on – people going over by fishing boat and playing they was Venezuelan citizen and getting big work. It had some test in Trinidad who reap big harvest off the racket. They used to get everybody who want to go and charge them plenty money and put them in a fishing boat. Then the fishing boat leave in the night and make a tack round the island and land the people up somewhere on the other coast that desolate, telling them that now they in Venezuela. By the time the people walk inland a little way they realise that they still in Trinidad, and they can't do anything about it, because the police was always looking out for people who want to go to Venezuela illegally.

Well Frederick had a friend name Parker who over there already, and Parker keep writing and saying how things good, that besides the money it have senoritas all over the place, that he living like a lord, and why Frederick don't try to come over, that he would help to get him fix up.

Work was hard to get in Trinidad at the time and Frederick decide to make the trip somehow. Only thing is that he don't know no Spanish. So he buy one of them books that say you could teach yourself, and he learn the language as best he could.

In the meantime he done join up a party of fellars what planning to go Venezuela through the back door. It had a creole fellar name Henry, who own the boat, another fellar name Charles who say he know Venezuela like the back of his hand but who didn't know a damn thing in truth, and a Indian name Lalsingh and a Chinese shopkeeper call Ling Ping, who say that he would open up a shop in one of them small village along the river.

All of them went down Icacos the night, by Columbus Bay, as down there is the nearest point to get across to the Main: fact, plenty time current catch hold of fishermen boat and land them up in Venezuela when they fishing in the Serpent's Mouth, and the Spanish government had was to have coastguards to send them back, or else they lock up the fishermen in a jail and throw away the key.

Well the current help out the party that night and they didn't have to do much rowing, and fo'day morning they find themselves up the river. But nobody know which part of the country they in: when they turn to Charles and ask him, Charles look around at the bush and jungle and say he never see this part of Venezuela in his born days.

Lalsingh and the Chinee man start to get frighten, because is only jungle all around them, like how in the films you see the star going up a river in Africa, and monkey and chimpanzee jumping in the branches of some powerful trees that hiding the sky from view.

Lalsingh and the Chinee shaking the cranky fishing boat and getting everybody frighten, because it have alligator making style in the water and only waiting for one of them to drop out, and same time Charles talking about a kind of small fish what does attack you and only leave bones when they finish.

On top of that, they ain't bring plenty rations. It only have four hops bread and two tin cornbeef and some dry coconut that they pick up on the beach at Icacos, and they can't land nowhere in the jungle that was all around them.

They went up the river for the whole day, and when night come they find a little place on the bank to pull up the boat. But some mosquito big like bee start to hum and dive around them, and they couldn't sleep at all, even though they light a fire with green bush for the smoke to drive them away.

Next morning nobody want to go anywhere, and a big argument start up about turning back and going up another branch of the river. Lalsingh and the Chinee want to go back to Trinidad, Charles saying that he would walk through the jungle, and Henry saying that is his boat and he going on, and Frederick saying yes Henry, you right boy, let we go on, we must reach some place what have people.

Well same time they arguing Charles spot a piece of meat hanging from a branch on a tree by the bank, and that was a sure sign that they near to a village, for the bush-Indians in that part of the country does hang out meat like that to get dry in the sun, and afterwards they salt it and it last for weeks.

Everybody grab paddle and oar and start to get into action. But they paddle up the river whole morning and can't see nobody. To make things worse, it now have a kind of vine growing under the water, and whenever they dip a paddle it sticking up in the vine and the boat won't go. So Frederick had was to stay up in front of the boat, and cut the vine with a cutlass Henry had.

Praise the Lord, in the afternoon they reach a village where some bush-Indian living. Courage return now and everybody talking big, about how they wasn't really frighten, that they did know all the time that they bound to reach a village.

Well the plan was that as soon as they reach a village they would split up, each man on his own. It have some worthless fellars in Venezuela who if they don't like your head would go and tell the police that you come to the country illegally, and Frederick was glad that he didn't tell any of the others what he plan to do.

He wait until the others scatter about and then he find out from the Indians how to get to the town, and by noon of the next day he was in true civilisation in the place where Parker living, and Parker was shaking hand and opening a big bottle of Spanish wine.

Frederick was tired and hungry but after eating Parker asking all kind of question about the people back home, asking if his grandmother still alive and if his Tanty does still go to see her. Frederick saying yes and no to all the questions, because he don't know anything much about Parker family in Trinidad. In fact, all he know is that Parker write and tell him to come to Venezuela, that he would help to get him fix up. So he cut short all the old-talk and ask Parker what it was he had to do now that he was in the country.

Parker tell Frederick that he had to get what they call a 'cedula', because that was the main thing, when you have that people does believe that you belong to the country, and you could get a work without too much trouble.

'You here a long time, and is all right for you to talk so,' Frederick say, 'but what happen, it ain't have no police?'

'Police! Boy, as long as you have money, you safe as a bat. Them police don't see you when you hide behind a dollar bill. But as you talk about that, it remind me that you have to get another business what call "libreta militar".'

'What that is? Man, you making this sound hard, after you promise to help me out.'

'Is a paper that say you finish do your service in the army. Over here everybody have to put in some time in the forces – if they find out that you ain't do none, they pull you out of your work and make you join up the army. Sometimes even though you have your papers they still take you away and make a lot of fuss.'

Frederick begin to think that things wasn't so rosy after all. 'H'mm, when you write me you didn't say anything about all that. You only say Yankee was giving work all about, and you could get a big work for me where you working.'

'Yes, yes,' Parker say, drinking wine as if he was the guest and not Frederick. 'Don't fret yourself, I will get you fix up. Tomorrow I sending you by a fellar name Enrique who will get all them papers for you, and then you wouldn't have a thing to worry about.'

So briss-briss the next morning Frederick hop in a bus to go to the City of Bolivar, which part he was to look for this fellar what name Enrique.

The bus drive a long time, and they even pass through a desert. Frederick didn't even know it had desert in that part of the world. And one time the driver had to get out and coax two cattle from off the road for the bus to go on.

When they get to the city everybody in the bus had to sign a book saying how long they intended to stay.

It had some sharp senoritas strolling about but Frederick attending strictly to business, and wouldn't allow himself to be distracted. Parker did tell him that Enrique always taking ease

in the park, so Frederick ask some boys who did pitching
marbles which part the park is, and the boys say up the road,
so Frederick went.

When he reach by there he see Enrique quite easily, for he was
a small Indian test with a wooden leg, wearing a khaki suit and
a peak cap like a ship officer. He was sitting down on a bench
with the wooden leg stretch out, like he ain't have a worry in
the world. But by the time Frederick could reach he get up
and start to hobble up the road.

Frederick went after him.

'Aye, Enrique, I have some business for you . . .' he begin
to say.

But Enrique play as if he ain't hear him at all.

Frederick go to talk again but same time Enrique turn his
head as if he vex and say, 'Don't talk to me here, you damn
fool. Keep walking. It have policemen all about the place.'

Frederick walk up the road a little bit and stand by a corner.
Enrique come and he looking all about, as if he 'fraid some
policeman would appear suddenly and arrest him. He ain't
looking at Frederick at all, is as if he talking in the air. He say
which part he living, and he tell Frederick to go there and wait
for him. And with that he hobble off.

When Frederick did left Trinidad he didn't bargain for all
this mystery action, but he decide that he in Venezuela already
and he best hads do what Enrique tell him.

He went to this house, and a fat Venezuelan woman open
the door, and he try out his Spanish and tell she that he had
business with Enrique, who tell him to come and wait. She tell
him to come inside and sit down.

Little later Enrique come in, bawling out about how the sun
so hot, and how things so hard with him these days, as if he
want Frederick to know in front how the position is.

Well the two of them begin to talk, and right away Frederick could tell that Enrique was a Trinidadian, though he play
as if he real stupid and didn't say so.

'Is Parker that send me to you,' Frederick say. 'I want to get this cedula business.'

'You is a Venezuelan?' Enrique ask. This time so, he like a different man to when he was by the park, he ain't frighten again, he like a detective asking question.

'No,' Frederick say.

'You damn stupid, you must say yes. You better get in the habit from now. You is a Venezuelan, a born Venezuelan.' Enrique stretch out the wooden leg and say, 'A-a-ah.' Then he say, as if he talking to himself, 'So Parker send you, eh! But he ain't send the two hundred bees he owe me a long time now?'

'I ain't know nothing about that,' Frederick get cagey right away.

Enrique grunt. 'If wasn't for me Parker see hell to remain in this country. I help that man out of plenty trouble. Now he have a big work with the Yankees, drawing American dollars, and he still won't pay me that money that he owe.'

Enrique pick up a magazine and begin to fan himself furiously, opening the top of his shirt and showing a hairy chest. 'Is how you come to this country?'

'Through the backdoor, like everybody else.'

'Is a good thing. That mean that nobody know you here. You could talk Spanish?'

'Yes.'

'You could talk it good? You don't stutter and fumble? It have some fellars who think they is parrot when it come to Spanish, but ask them to say something and they dumb.'

'I does talk it good.'

'So what is your name?'

'Rafael Gomes,' Frederick say. That was a name that Parker did give him to use.

'Rafael Gomes,' Enrique repeat. 'It not so bad, is a good Venezuelan name. How much money you bring?'

Frederick start to get cagey again. 'I only have about two hundred bees that I borrow to pay back when I start to work.'

'Two hundred bees! Is that self that Parker have for me. You sure you ain't trying a fast one? I know Parker good, you know. If you try anything with me, boy, monkey smoke your pipe!'

'Man, I new in this country, you think I would be so foolish?'

Enrique did getting excited and leaning forward, but now he relax. He say, 'Ah, you only wasting my time. Two hundred bees! That not enough at all. You better go back and come back in a month when you have more money. Things bad this side now. The Big Man who does fix these papers for me say they might transfer him at any time. Things getting warm. A lot of fellars like you does come and cry big water and bawl and ask me to help them out, and promise to come back and pay the rest, but when they peel off from here I don't see them again at all. You think I could go to the Big Man and talk about "balance"?'

'I know how you mean,' Frederick say quickly, realising the position was getting tough, 'but I won't mamaguile you. If the two hundred I have not enough, as soon as I start to work I go pay you the rest.'

Well same time as Frederick talking, three chicken and two pig walk in the room from the backyard.

Enrique sit up and pelt the crutch after them, and he begin to fire some curse in Spanish.

'I tired tell that damn woman to keep the back door shut. But as if she deaf sometimes. She too ignorant.' He look at Frederick and wink. 'Is all right, she can't understand a thing we talking about, she don't know English.'

Then as if he remember something he say suddenly, '*Como se bama?*'

He thought he would of catch Frederick offguard but praise the Lord that was one of the phrase that Frederick learn from the Spanish book and he fire back at him, 'Rafael Gomes'.

Enrique smile and relax. He say, 'It look like you know something, you look like an all-right fellar. I will do something big for you.' And he get up and hobble to the next room.

Frederick hear him muttering saying how his wife does misplace every damn thing that he put down.

When he come back, he say, 'I have a birth certificate here. Don't ask me how I get it. It really for a fellar who promise to come back, but is three weeks now and I ain't see him. I go let you have it, but you have to change your name.'

He hand Frederick the paper and tell him to read it, and Frederick see as if it look like the real thing, it have all kind of government stamp and signature on it.

Enrique peep over his shoulder. 'You see where it say that this Jose Morales is a illegitimate child – and that is you, get that straight. You don't know your father at all, and your mother was a washerwoman. Remember the date and the place that you born, and remember your age, don't go mixing things up, or else you put all of we in a jail where they lock you up and throw away the key.'

'But what about the cedula thing?' Frederick ask.

'It too late for that today, and besides you have to learn these new details good. Tomorrow please God I go take you to the office, and you will get fix up. And another thing. If afterwards anybody ask you how much you pay for your cedula, the answer is three bees, three bees in stamps. That is what the government charge, don't play powerful foolish and say three hundred bees like some stupid fellars, because right there you will stick yourself big.'

The two of them went on talking for a while, then Frederick realise that he ain't have no place to stay for the night, and he ask Enrique if he know of any cheap place.

Enrique say that if he could sleep in a hammock, he could spent the night. Frederick agree, but afterwards he was wishing that he did go somewhere else, because all night Enrique keep firing questions at him, to make sure he know all the answers what to tell the people in the office.

Next morning, as soon as they get out of the house, Enrique start to get on again like a big spy in a film. He pull Frederick by the side of the road and say, 'Listen, I going upstairs in the office, and you wait across the road. When you see me look out the window and wipe my face with this handkerchief...' he pull out a yellow one, 'that is the signal for you to come and ask for the cedula. Hand them the birth certificate that I give you. But if you see me wipe my face with this handkerchief...' Enrique pull a red one from his back pocket, 'that is the signal to make races, get out of the city, go as far as you could and never stop.'

'Yes,' Frederick say, 'but I don't see no reason for all of this big drama.'

'Don't mind me,' Enrique say, 'I know my business. You just do as I say. Now after you get fix up, go downstairs where they have a café. Order a beer and start to drink it slow. The Big Man will come to see you there, and when he shake your hand you must slip him the two hundred bees. You got all of that?'

'All right,' Frederick say.

'And if you see any policemen around, don't stand up one place, move around as if you seeing the sights.'

With that Enrique went into the office and left Frederick on the other side of the road.

Cold sweat take Frederick as he stand up there waiting, imagining all kinds of things. He don't know how long he was there, but suddenly he spot Enrique by the window looking out. Enrique was wiping his face with a handkerchief.

Frederick look good and panic take him as he see that Enrique was wiping his face with two handkerchief, one red and one yellow. What that mean?

He just about to make races out of town when Enrique drop the red one and begin wiping hard with the yellow one.

Man must take chances to live, Frederick decide, and with that he make up a brave mind and went in the place.

It had a test sit down behind a desk and he start to ask Frederick all sorts of questions, and Frederick don't know where the Spanish coming from but he giving the test as much as he taking.

Well the Lord was with him, the test give him a paper and say that it would do until he get the real cedula from the office of the Ministry in Caracas.

By the time Frederick get the paper in his hand he bounce back outside, ready to make races out of town and forget Enrique and Big Man and everything. But across the road he see Enrique stand up, like if he know what going on in Frederick mind, and he wave his hand in the direction of the café.

Frederick went in the café and order a beer, studying what to do.

Suddenly a hand fall on his shoulder and he hear a fellar say, '*Amigo mio, que tal como estas.*'

Frederick nearly dead with fright, but all the same he keep his head and he turn to see who the fellar was.

It was the same test who give him the paper upstairs.

Trying hard to keep cool, Frederick say quickly, '*Hasta la vista, amigo, estoy muy ocupados en este momento,*' and with that he shake the fellar hand and palm off a bill that was worth only twenty bees, and walk out fast, leaving half the beer in the glass.

When he get outside he play as if he ain't see Enrique waiting on the other side and start to walk up the road quick.

Enrique call out, 'Aye! Aye man! Wait for me!'

But Frederick start to hustle fast, because he know that poor Enrique only have one foot and could never catch up with him. He look back and see Enrique hobbling fast with the wooden leg, but he had the chances of a snowball in hell of catching up with Frederick.

Two weeks later Frederick get a work with a big American oil company as Jose Morales, Venezuelan citizen, bastard son of a washerwoman.

As for Enrique? Well he must be still down the Main fixing up all kind of false paper for the boys that manage to come over, and moaning that nobody ever pay him for all the chances he take. Is either that, or else the law catch up with him and they put him in that jail where they lock you up and throw away the key.

Holiday in Five Rivers

WHEN IT WAS the last day of school Popo put his copybook and food-carrier in the satchel his mother had made for him from a piece of coloured cotton, and he waited at the gate for Govind, his big brother, and together they took the stony trail that led four miles over hill and valley to Five Rivers.

The road didn't seem as stony as usual, because the school was going to be closed a long time for repairs.

Popo was full of excitement.

'Plenty holiday, we will have time to do plenty things.' Govind, twelve years old, was just as enthusiastic, but all the same he said to Popo:

'Plenty things, yes! But I warning you from in front, that I don't want you hanging around my tail all the time. You still a little boy, and you must play with children your age.'

'I won't do anything, Govind.' The little boy held on to his brother's hand and looked up entreatingly. 'I just want to be with you, because you always doing brave things, and I getting big now, too besides.'

Govind flung Popo's grip off his hand. 'Ah, you too small to have any sense, you always making noise, or starting to cry and say you want to go home. You remember the time when we did went to thief in Procop garden? What happen? When the watchman see us, everybody run, but you sit down and start to cry.'

'But that was long time,' Popo walked backwards in front of his brother to talk face to face. 'I promise you this time I will do whatever you say. And you remember the time when Pa was putting a cock and some rice at the crossroads to work obeah, ain't it was I who did tell you about it?'

'Ah, and you remember the time when Pa did ask who it was that burst the strap for the donkey saddle, ain't it was you who tell him that it was me?'

'But you remember the time when you did run away from school to go and fish cascadura in the river, I didn't say nothing then, though.'

They walked along the rugged trail, trading memories in a fierce argument, until at last, as they got to the small hill over-looking Five Rivers, Govind said:

'All right, but I warning you in front, the first time you make a mistake, I not going to take you anywhere where I go.'

From where they were now, the village looked like it was in a basin at their feet. High green hills, covered with lush vegetation, surrounded the village, and when it was the season of pouis these flowers showed like yellow blobs decorating the hillsides. But there was always colour besides the stagnant green, for if immortelles' crimson blossoms were absent here and there were blooms of perennial wild tropical plants.

Far in the Northern Range a river started, and when it got to the valley of Five Rivers it broke up because of the lay of the land, and there were five little streams which flowed near the village, giving it its name.

The peasants lived simply, out of touch with happenings in other parts of Trinidad, in a little world where food and shelter and a drink in Chin's shop on Saturday night were all the requisites for existence.

In that one shop anything from a bottle of rum to a safety pin could be bought. It was owned and run by Chin, a fat Chinaman. Chin was so much in demand that he never left the shop except to visit the nearest town on Sundays to see some friends and have a smoke of opium. When he did that, the shop remained closed until his return late on Monday morning. So that on a Saturday night every man, woman and child was there, and it was like a regular bazaar with shouting and drinking and smoking and gossiping.

When they had indulged in all the usual activities, like hunting birds and squirrels or bathing in one of the streams, Govind and Popo began to find the holidays dull. These were things they did all the time, school or no school.

Then one morning Chin spread a canvas awning in front of the shop to keep out the rays of the sun. Under this awning there was a wooden veranda where sometimes women sold sweets and cakes.

When Chin did that, More Lazy decided to migrate from under the spreading samaan tree in the centre of the village and go to live on Chin's veranda. This transplanting of his body caused More Lazy some concern, as it entailed the use of his own energy to walk the hundred-odd yards to the shop. But for some time he had noticed that the samaan tree protected him from the heat only in the morning. From noon, as the sun travelled west, it threw rays under the tree and on to More Lazy where he lay dozing.

Govind and Popo and the other children stopped pitching marbles in amazement as More Lazy got up and stretched under the samaan tree.

'Look! Look More Lazy getting up!' they shouted, and they began to tease the old negro.

In the whole of Five Rivers, or the whole of Trinidad for that matter, there was not another man lazier than More Lazy, and when he moved from under the samaan tree it was the subject of much conversation. They have it to say in the village that once Mr Dosanto, the plantation overseer, went into the shop to buy a drink, and on leaving accidentally dropped a dollar bill near to where More Lazy was, not knowing anything. They say it fell within a foot of More Lazy, and all he had to do was stretch out his hand and put it away without saying a word. But instead he kept an eye on it and waited until someone was passing by, then he asked for the person to bend down and pick it up for him, please.

It was only once a year that he stirred and came to life. That was during Carnival, the two-day festival before Ash Wednesday. More Lazy would bestir himself and journey into the capital of Port of Spain to take part in the celebrations. And while others were content to disguise themselves as pirates or Arabian sheikhs, he, strangely enough, had to enjoy himself in a more active impersonation, and would get someone to team up with him to play 'police and thief', he playing the part of a policeman chasing a thief through the streets of the city.

Accompanied by jeers and taunts from the children, More Lazy accomplished the journey to Chin's shop and established himself in a corner with a loud sigh, his body falling wearily to the ground.

The children stood at a distance and teased him, and Govind threw a stone. But More Lazy was unresponsive and they went off to pitch marbles again.

The dry season came and the boys set traps for ground-doves. In the brown bush, they bent limbs and made bows, and attached strings with loops.

But Govind tired of pastimes which didn't call for risks, and for two days, whenever Popo came near to him, he pushed his small brother away, sneering at any suggestion he offered to pass the time away as being childish and not worth the effort.

Then Popo surprised him by saying, 'I make friends with More Lazy, though.'

'How you do that?' Govind wanted to know, for they were always teasing the old man and he in turn threatened them if they came within reach.

'Oh, I do one or two little things for him, and now he and I is good friends, he tell me a secret.'

'What secret?' Govind asked disinterestedly, wishing with all his heart that a bush fire would break out or something.

'Well, it not really a secret. But he tell me a trick we could play on Jagroop.'

Jagroop was an old Hindu who lived on one of the hills, about half a mile up, where the forest was so thick that one was taken aback to come across the sudden clearing where his hut was. Jagroop had cut away the bush and built the hut himself, using bamboo from the river banks and palm leaves to thatch the roof. He made the walls with mud reinforced with dry grass and shrubs. Sometimes hunters passed near to Jagroop's place in the night, and he used to be so angry that he threatened to poison the river water and kill out the whole village unless they stopped trespassing on his property.

Every Saturday he passed through the village with the panniers of his donkey laden with fruits and vegetables. He never stopped on his way out to the bigger village of Sans Souci. He said the people in Five Rivers were too cheap, that he couldn't make any profit selling to them.

But when he got back in the evening he would regularly tie his donkey outside Chin's shop and stand up for a few minutes to curse More Lazy, saying that it was a shame that he slept all day while other people had to work hard. Then he would enter the shop and proceed to get drunk.

It was a weekly pattern with him. He was tight with his money, no one knew what he did with all the money he made trading. He didn't spend it all on rum, for after one bottle he was so drunk that some kindly villager had to put him on the donkey and send him home.

'Well, tell me, what trick it is?' Govind asked.

'First you much promise to take me with you,' Popo said.

'All right. What is the trick?'

Popo went close to his brother although they were alone and whispered in his ear. Govind's face brightened.

'Tonight self we will do it. You and me, and Lal and Harry could come too if they like.'

That night the boys stole an empty coffin and placed it in front of Jagroop's hut. They screamed and made all sorts of horrifying noises and hid in the bushes to see what would happen.

Jagroop flung open the door, cursing loudly in Hindi. When he saw the coffin, instead of backing away in fear he gave it a kick. Then he went inside and came back with a cutlass and he hacked the coffin to pieces, swearing all the time.

'Ah, that was a stupid idea,' Govind said afterwards, 'he didn't do anything, he wasn't frighten at all.'

They were all disappointed at the result, and a few days later when Popo told Govind, 'More Lazy tell me another trick to play on Jagroop,' Govind said:

'Ah, you never have any good ideas. I going to fish with Lal, and I don't want you to come.'

'But listen, this is a good trick .. well, it not a trick really. Is to look for treasure.'

'Treasure? Who would have treasure in Five Rivers, where everybody so poor?'

'Well, don't be so impatienate, man. But promise to take me first.'

'All right, but I hope is something good More Lazy tell you this time.'

'You know how Jagroop always selling plenty provisions, and how he is a stingy man. More Lazy say how he sure that Jagroop have plenty money hide up some place, and that we could look for it. He say that he would go himself, but is only that he does be so tired.'

'You mean lazy,' Govind said. But he thought about the idea, and the more he thought about it, the more appealing it seemed to him.

'All right! We will look all about for it!'

Govind felt it was a challenge to his ability, and in a short time he had mustered a gang of boys and they set about to look for the Indian's money.

Likely spots in and around the village were dug up. One Saturday evening while Jagroop was getting drunk Govind even ventured into the hut and ripped away the floor-boards. They set a night and day watch on Jagroop, spying on him as he worked on his plot or pottered about the yard.

But search high, search low, there was no discovering where the Indian had hidden his money, though More Lazy, having nothing to do, would get up after a doze and say he had dreamt where the money was hidden, and send them off on a wild goose chase.

For a week they kept at it, and then Govind said:

'Ah, that was another stupid idea. We can't find out where Jagroop have that money hide.'

The dry season was now at its height. The five streams around the village were mere trickles, not more than a foot wide or a couple of inches deep in places, and the villagers had to dig canals for the water to flow into one main channel.

Even More Lazy seemed affected, and he now lay with an earthen goblet of water and a tin can near him, so he could ask Popo to pour him a drink to quench his thirst.

It happened that most of the fruit trees around were bare except for a mango tree in Jagroop's garden which looked like it had sucked all the life from the other trees, for it was in full fruit, and from a distance the boys could see the red mangoes dangling on their stems.

Govind planned an 'attack' on this tree, so one morning with the leaves so dry and crisp they crackled like shells underfoot, he and Popo crept into the garden.

There was no sign of Jagroop, and this roused rather than allayed their fear. However, they managed to get behind the hut—making a wide circle to avoid it—and right under the mango tree.

Govind hoisted Popo up and soon they were at the top of the tree feasting on the fruit, Popo having brought a penknife and pepper and salt with which to eat the green ones.

They had filled their pockets and bosoms and were just about to descend when Popo held Govind's arm in a tight grasp and pointed.

Below them the bush was so thick they couldn't see if someone was passing below, all they saw was the bushes shake.

It was Jagroop. Even though he was completely hidden he was walking in a sort of half crouch, a cutlass and tin clutched to his chest while one hand cleared the way of brambles. He stopped where one of the streams crawled through the land, and glancing all around, sat down on the bank and wet his cutlass and began to sharpen it on a stone.

He was now clearly seen by the boys, and it appeared to them that he was only pretending, or 'playing possum' as they used to say. For all the time he was watching the bushes, like a deer which had smelt man but wasn't sure where he was. And the boys got real scared, for it looked like he knew all the time they were up in the mango tree, and it looked too, the easy way he was sitting, that he was only waiting for them to climb down to give chase with his cutlass.

They scarcely dared breathe, and Govind could feel Popo's fingers squeezing and relaxing, squeezing and relaxing on his arm.

'You think he see we?' Popo's whisper was hot in Govind's ear.

'Let we wait and see what he go do,' Govind whispered back, no less afraid than his little brother.

Half an hour passed. Jagroop was humming a Hindi song as he moved the cutlass to and fro on the stone. The cutlass must have been as sharp as a razor, yet he went on. He struck it lightly at a hanging bamboo leaf. Then he tested the blade again by shaving an inch or two of hair off his leg.

And that seemed to satisfy him, for he got up at last. Near to a large slab of rock which jutted out from the bank he stood up for a minute. Then muttering to himself he gathered stones, and he damned the thin trickle of water, digging earth from the bank with his cutlass.

And when the water ceased to flow, he began to dig in the bed of the stream itself.

The boys could see beads of perspiration glistening on his

dark skin as he dug and dug, stopping at sudden moments and cocking his head sideways as dry leaves rustled or a dove flew noisily in the bush.

For another half an hour they hung suspended, as it were, on the branches of the mango tree.

Then Jagroop stopped digging and reached into the hole with his hands.

He brought out two tins and he sat down and opened them.

Sunlight fell on silver. Hundreds of shillings and two-shillings and half-crown pieces. They glinted and the boys could hear the ring as he let them trickle through his fingers and fall back into the tins.

Jagroop chuckled as he played with the money, entirely engrossed in his hoarding.

Govind saw now why they had been unable to discover the hiding place. Who would have dreamed of digging in the bed of a flowing stream? Not even More Lazy himself. Now, all the Indian had to do was bury the money and fill the hole firmly with stones and earth, and break the dam and the water would flow over the spot and keep the secret.

It was too good. It was too clever. They couldn't contain themselves. They were just bursting to reveal the secret.

Scrambling down the mango tree with an exciting elation, Govind and Popo set up a great shouting to give themselves courage, and jettisoning mangoes left and right from their pockets and bosoms, ran pell-mell down the hill to the village.

Cane is Bitter

IN FEBRUARY they began to reap the cane in the undulating fields at Cross Crossing estate in the southern part of Trinidad. 'Crop time coming boy, plenty work for everybody,' men in the village told one another. They set about sharpening their cutlasses on grinding stones, ceasing only when they tested the blades with their thumb-nails and a faint ping! quivered in the air. Or they swung the cutlass at a drooping leaf and cleaved it. But the best test was when it could shave the hairs off your leg.

Everyone was happy in Cross Crossing as work loomed up in the way of their idleness, for after the planting of the cane there was hardly any work until the crop season. They laughed and talked more and the children were given more liberty than usual, so they ran about the barracks and played hide and seek in those canefields which had not yet been fired to make the reaping easier. In the evening, when the dry trash was burnt away from the stalks of sweet juice, they ran about clutching the black straw which rose on the wind: people miles away knew when crop season was on for the burnt trash was blown a great distance away. The children smeared one another on the face and laughed at the black streaks. It wouldn't matter now if their exertions made them hungry, there would be money to buy flour and rice when the men worked in the fields, cutting and carting the cane to the weighing-bridge.

In a muddy pond about two hundred yards east of the settlement, under the shade of spreading *laginette* trees, women washed clothes and men bathed mules and donkeys and hog-cattle. The women beat the clothes with stones to get them clean, squatting by the banks, their skirts drawn tight against the back of their thighs, their saris retaining grace of arrangement on their shoulders even in that awkward position. Naked children splashed about in the pond, hitting the water with their hands and shouting when the water shot up in the air at different angles, and trying to make brief rainbows in the sunlight with the spray. Rays of the morning sun came slantways from halfway up in the sky, casting the shadow of trees on the pond, and playing on the brown bodies of the children.

Ramlal came to the pond and sat on the western bank, so that he squinted into the sunlight. He dipped his cutlass in the water and began to sharpen it on the end of a rock on which his wife Rookmin was beating clothes. He was a big man, and in earlier days was reckoned handsome. But work in the fields had not only tanned his skin to a deep brown but actually changed his features. His nose had a slight hump just above the nostrils, and the squint in his eyes was there even in the night, as if he was peering all the time, though his eyesight was remarkable. His teeth were stained brown with tobacco, so brown that when he laughed it blended with the colour of his face, and you only saw the lips stretched wide and heard the rumble in his throat.

Rookmin was frail but strong as most East Indian women. She was not beautiful, but it was difficult to take any one feature of her face and say it was ugly. Though she was only thirty-six, hard work and the bearing of five children had taken toll. Her eyes were black and deceptive, and perhaps she might have been unfaithful to Ramlal if the idea had ever occurred to her. But like most of the Indians in the country districts, half her desires and emotions were never given a chance to live, her life dedicated to wresting an existence for herself and her family. But as if she knew the light she threw from her eyes, she had a habit of shutting them whenever she was emotional. Her breasts sagged from years of suckling. Her hands were wrinkled and callous. The toes of her feet were spread wide from walking without any footwear whatsoever: she never had need for a pair of shoes because she never left the village.

She watched Ramlal out of the corner of her eye as he sharpened the cutlass, sliding the blade to and fro on the rock. She knew he had something on his mind, the way how he had come silently and sat near to her pretending that he could add to the keenness of his razor-sharp cutlass. She waited for him to speak, in an oriental respectfulness. But from the attitude of both of them, it wasn't possible to tell that they were about to converse, or even that they were man and wife. Rookmin went on washing clothes, turning the garments over and over as she pounded them on a flat stone, and Ramlal squinted his eyes and looked at the sun.

At last, after five minutes or so, Ramlal spoke.

'Well, that boy Romesh coming home tomorrow. Is six months since last he come home. This time, I make up my mind, he not going back.'

Rookmin went on scrubbing, she did not even look up.

'You see how city life change the boy. When he was here the last time, you see how he was talking about funny things?'

Rookmin held up a tattered white shirt and looked at the sun through it.

'But you think he will agree to what we going to do?' she asked. 'He must be learning all sorts of new things, and this time might be worse than last time. Suppose he want to take creole wife?'

'But you mad or what? That could never happen. Ain't we make all arrangement with Sampath for Doolsie to married him? Anyway,' he went on, 'is all your damn fault in the first place, wanting to send him for education in the city. You see what it cause? The boy come like a stranger as soon as he start to learn all those funny things they teach you in school, talking about poetry and books and them funny things. I did never want to send him for education, but is you who make me do it.'

'Education is a good thing,' Rookmin said, without intonation. 'One day he might come lawyer or doctor, and all of we would live in a big house in the town, and have servants to look after we.'

'That is only foolish talk,' Ramlal said. 'You think he would remember we when he come a big man? And besides, by that time you and me both dead. And besides, the wedding done plan and everything already.'

'Well, if he married Doolsie everything might work out.'

'How you mean if? I had enough of all this business. He have to do what I say, else I put him out and he never come here again. Doolsie father offering big dowry, and afterwards the both of them could settle on the estate and he could forget all that business.'

Rookmin was silent. Ramlal kept testing the blade with his nail, as if he were fascinated by the pinging sound, as if he were trying to pick out a tune.

But in fact he was thinking, thinking about the last time his son Romesh had come home . . .

It was only his brothers and sisters, all younger than himself, who looked at Romesh with wonder, wanting to ask him questions about the world outside the canefields and the village. Their eyes expressed their thoughts, but out of some curious embarrassment they said nothing. In a way, this brother was a stranger, someone who lived far away in the city, only coming home once or twice a year to visit them. They were noticing a change, a distant look in his eyes. Silently, they drew aside from him, united in their lack of understanding. Though Romesh never spoke of the great things he was learning, or tried to show off his knowledge, the very way he bore himself now, the way he watched the cane moving in the wind was alien to their feelings. When they opened the books he had brought, eager to see the pictures, there were only pages and pages of words, and they couldn't read. They watched him in the night, crouching in the corner, the book on the floor near to the candle, reading. That alone made him different, set him apart. They thought he was going to be a pundit, or a priest, or something extraordinary. Once his sister had asked: 'What do you read so much about, *bhai*?' and Romesh looked at her with a strange look and said, 'To tell you, you wouldn't understand. But have patience, a time will come soon, I hope, when all of you will learn to read and write.' Then Hari, his brother, said, 'Why do you feel we will not understand? What is wrong with our brains? Do you think because you go to school in the city that you are better than us? Because you get the best clothes to wear, and shoes to put on your feet, because you get favour from *bap* and *mai*?' Romesh said quickly, '*Bhai*, it is not that. It is only that I have left our village, and have learned about many things which you do not know about. The whole world goes ahead in all fields, in politics, in science, in art. Even now the governments in the West Indies are talking about federating the islands, and then what will happen to the Indians in this island? But we must not quarrel, soon all of us will have a chance.' But Hari was not impressed. He turned to his father and mother and said: 'See how he has changed. He don't want to play no games anymore, he don't want to work in the fields, he is too much of a bigshot to use a cutlass. His brothers and sisters are fools, he don't want to talk to them because they won't understand. He don't even want to eat we food again, this morning I see he ain't touch the *baghi*. No. We have to get chicken for him, and the cream from all the cows in the village. Yes, that is what. And who it is does sweat for him to get pretty shirt to wear in Port of Spain?' He held up one of the girls' arms and spanned it with his fingers. 'Look how thin she is. All that is for you to be a big man, and now you scorning your own family?' Romesh got up from the floor and faced them. His eyes burned fiercely, and he looked like the pictures of Indian gods the children had seen in the village hall. 'You are all wrong!' he cried in a ringing voice, 'surely you, *bap*, and you, *mai*, the years must have taught you that you must make

a different life for your children, that you must free them from
ignorance and the wasting away of their lives? Do you want
them to suffer as you have?' Rookmin looked like she was
going to say something, but instead she shut her eyes tight.
Ramlal said: 'Who tell you we suffer? We bring children in
the world and we happy.' But Romesh went on, 'And what
will the children do? Grow up in the village here, without
learning to read and write? There are schools in San Fernando,
surely you can send them there to learn about different things
besides driving a mule and using a cutlass? Oh *bap*, we are such
a backward people, all the others move forward to better lives,
and we lag behind believing that what is to be, will be. All over
Trinidad, in the country districts, our people toil on the land
and reap the cane. For years it has been so, years in the same
place, learning nothing new, accepting our fate like animals.
Political men come from India and give speeches in the city.
They speak of better things, they tell us to unite and strive for
a greater goal. And what does it mean to you? Nothing. You
are content to go hungry, to see your children run about naked,
emaciated, grow up dull and stupid, slaves to your own indifference. You do not even pretend an interest in the Legislative Council. I remember why you voted for Pragsingh last
year, it was because he gave you ten dollars – did I not see it
for myself? It were better that we returned to India than stay
in the West Indies and live such a low form of existence.' The
family watched Romesh wide-eyed. Ramlal sucked his clay
pipe noisily. Rookmin held her youngest daughter in her lap,
picking her head for lice, and now and then shutting her eyes
so the others wouldn't see what she was thinking. 'There is
only one solution,' Romesh went on, 'we must educate the
children, open up new worlds in their minds, stretch the horizon of their thoughts . . .' Suddenly he stopped. He realised
that for some time now they weren't listening, his words didn't
make any sense to them. Perhaps he was going about this the
wrong way, he would have to find some other way of explain-

ing how he felt. And was he sufficiently equipped in himself to propose vast changes in the lives of the people? It seemed to him then how small he was, how there were so many things he didn't know. All the books he'd read, the knowledge he'd lapped up hungrily in the city, listening to the politicians making speeches in the square – all these he mustered to his assistance. But it was as if his brain was too small, it was like putting your mouth in the sea and trying to drink all the water. Wearily, like an old man who had tried to prove his point merely by repeating, 'I am old, I should know,' Romesh sat down on the floor, and there was silence in the hut, a great silence, as if the words he'd spoken had fled the place and gone outside with the wind and the cane.

And so after he had gone back to the city his parents discussed the boy, and concluded that the only thing to save his senses was to marry him off. 'You know he like Sampath daughter from long time, and she is a hard-working girl, she go make good wife for him.' Rookmin had said. Ramlal had seen Sampath and everything was fixed. Everybody in the village knew of the impending wedding . . .

Romesh came home the next day. He had some magazines and books under his arm, and a suitcase in his hand. There was no reception for him; everyone who could work was out in the fields.

He was as tall as the canes on either side of the path on which he walked. He sniffed the smell of burning cane, but he wasn't overjoyful at coming home. He had prepared for this, prepared for the land on which he had toiled as a child, the thatched huts, the children running naked in the sun. He knew that these were things not easily forgotten which he had to forget. But he saw how waves of wind rippled over the seas of cane and he wondered vaguely about big things like happiness and love and poetry, and how they could fit into the poor, toiling lives the villagers led.

Romesh met his sisters at home. They greeted him shyly but he held them in his arms and cried, '*Beti*, do you not know your own brother?' And they laughed and hung their heads on his shoulder.

'Everybody gone to work,' one girl said, 'and we cooking food to carry. Pa and Ma was looking out since early this morning, they say to tell you if you come to come in the fields.'

Romesh looked around the hut in which he had grown up. It seemed to him that if he had come back home after ten years, there would still be the old table in the centre of the room, its feet sunk in the earthen floor, the black pots and pans hanging on nails near the window. Nothing would change. They would plant the cane, and when it grew and filled with sweet juice cut it down for the factory. The children would waste away their lives working with their parents. No schooling, no education, no widening of experience. It was the same thing the man had lectured about in the public library three nights before in Port of Spain. The most they would learn would be to wield a cutlass expertly, or drive the mule cart to the railway line swiftly so that before the sun went down they would have worked sufficiently to earn more than their neighbours.

With a sigh like an aged man Romesh opened his suitcase and took out a pair of shorts and a polo shirt. He put these on and put the suitcase away in a corner. He wondered where would be a safe place to put his books. He opened the suitcase again and put them in.

It was as if, seeing the room in which he had argued and quarrelled with the family on his last visit, he lost any happiness he might have had coming back this time. A feeling of depression overcame him.

It lasted as he talked with his sisters as they prepared food to take to the fields. Romesh listened how they stumbled with words, how they found it difficult to express themselves. He thought how regretful it was that they couldn't go to school.

He widened the thought and embraced all the children in the village, growing up with such little care, running naked in the mud with a piece of *roti* in their hands, missing out on all the things that life should stand for.

But when the food was ready and they set off for the fields, with the sun in their eyes making them blind, he felt better. He would try to be happy with them, while he was here. No more preaching. No more voicing of opinion on this or that.

Other girls joined his sisters as they walked, all carrying food. When they saw Romesh they blushed and tittered, and he wondered what they were whispering about among themselves.

There were no effusive greetings. Sweating as they were, their clothes black with the soot of burnt canes, their bodies caught in the motions of their work, they just shouted out, and Romesh shouted back. Then Ramlal dropped the reins and jumped down from his cart. He curved his hand like a boomerang and swept it over his face. The soot from his sleeves smeared his face as he wiped away the sweat.

Rookmin came up and opened tired arms to Romesh. '*Beta*,' she cried as she felt his strong head on her breast. She would have liked to stay like that, drawing his strength and vitality into her weakened body, and closing her eyes so her emotions wouldn't show.

'*Beta*,' his father said, 'you getting big, you looking strong.' They sat down to eat on the grass. Romesh was the only one who appeared cool, the others were flushed, the veins standing out on their foreheads and arms.

Romesh asked if it was a good crop.

'Yes *beta*,' Ramlal said, 'is a good crop, and plenty work for everybody. But this year harder than last year, because rain begin to fall early, and if we don't hurry up with the work, it will be too much trouble for all of us. The overseer come yesterday, and he say a big bonus for the man who do the most work. So everybody working hard for that bonus. Two of my mules sick, but I have to work them, I can't help. We trying to get the bonus.'

After eating Ramlal fished a cigarette zoot from his pocket and lit it carefully. First greetings over, he had nothing more to tell his son, for the time being anyway.

Romesh knew they were all remembering the last visit, and the things he had said then. This time he wasn't going to say anything, he was just going to have a holiday and enjoy it, and return to school in the city refreshed.

He said, 'Hari, I bet I could cut more canes than you.'

Hari laughed. 'Even though I work the whole morning already is a good bet. You must be forget to use *poya*, your hands so soft and white now.'

That is the way life is, Ramlal thought as Romesh took his cutlass. Education, school, chut! It was only work put a *roti* in your belly, only work that brought money. The marriage would change Romesh. And he felt a pride in his heart as his son spat on the blade.

The young men went to a patch of burnt canes. The girls came too, standing by to pile the fallen stalks of sweet juice into heaps, so that they could be loaded quickly and easily on to the carts and raced to the weighing-bridge.

Cane fell as if a machine were at work. The blades swung in the air, glistened for a moment in the sunlight, and descended on the stalks near the roots. Though the work had been started as a test of speed, neither of them moved ahead of the other. Sometimes Romesh paused until Hari came abreast, and sometimes Hari waited a few canes for Romesh. Once they looked at each other and laughed, the sweat on their faces getting into their mouths. There was no more enmity on Hari's part: seeing his brother like this, working, was like the old days when they worked side by side at all the chores which filled the day.

Everybody turned to in the field striving to outwork the

others, for each wanted the bonus as desperately as his neighbour. Sometimes the women and the girls laughed or made jokes to one another, but the men worked silently. And the crane on the weighing-bridge creaked and took load after load. The labourer manipulating it grumbled: there was no bonus for him, though his wage was more than that of the cane-cutters.

When the sun set all stopped work as if by signal. And in Ramlal's hut that night there was laughter and song. Everything was all right, they thought. Romesh was his natural self again, the way he swung that cutlass! His younger sisters and brother had never really held anything against him, and now that Hari seemed pleased, they dropped all embarrassment and made fun. 'See *bhai*, I make *meetai* especially for you,' his sister said, offering the sweetmeat.

'He work hard, he deserve it,' Hari agreed, and he looked at his brother almost with admiration.

Afterwards, when Ramlal was smoking and Rookmin was searching in the youngest girl's head for lice ('put pitch-oil, that will kill them,' Ramlal advised) Romesh said he was going to pay Doolsie a visit.

There was a sudden silence. Rookmin shut her eyes, the children stopped playing, and Ramlal coughed over his pipe

'Well, what is the matter?' Romesh asked, looking at their faces.

'Well, now,' Ramlal began, and stopped to clear his throat. 'Well now, you know that is our custom, that a man shouldn't go to pay visit to the girl he getting married . . .'

'What!' Romesh looked from face to face. The children shuffled their feet and began to be embarrassed at the stranger's presence once more.

Ramlal spoke angrily. 'Remember this is your father's house! Remember the smaller ones! Careful what you say, you must give respect! You not expect to get married one day, eh? Is a good match we make, boy, you will get good dowry, and you could live in the village and forget them funny things you learning in the city.'

'So it has all been arranged,' Romesh said slowly. 'That is why everybody looked at me in such a strange way in the fields. My life already planned for me, my path pointed out – cane, labour, boy children, and the familiar village of Cross Crossing.' His voice had dropped lower, as if he had been speaking to himself, but it rose again as he addressed his mother: 'And you, *mai*, you have helped them do this to me? You whose idea it was to give me an education?'

Rookmin shut her eyes and spoke. 'Is the way of our people, is we custom from long time. And you is Indian? The city fool your brains, but you will get back accustom after you married and have children.'

Ramlal got up from where he was squatting on the floor, and faced Romesh. 'You have to do what we say,' he said loudly. 'Ever since you in the city, we notice how you change. You forgetting custom and how we Indian people does live. And too besides, money getting short. We want help on the estate. The garden want attention, and nobody here to see about the cattle and them. And no work after crop, too besides.'

'Then I can go to school in San Fernando,' Romesh said desperately. 'If there is no money to pay the bus, I will walk. The government schools are free, you do not have to pay to learn.'

'You will married and have boy children,' Ramlal said, 'and you will stop answering your *bap* . . .'

'Hai! Hai!' Drivers urged their carts in the morning sun, and whips cracked crisply on the air. Dew still clung to the grass as workers took to the fields to do as much as they could before the heat of the sun began to tell.

Romesh was still asleep when the others left. No one woke him; they moved about the hut in silence. No one spoke. The boys went to harness the mules, one of the girls to milk the cows and the other was busy in the kitchen.

When Romesh got up he opened his eyes in full awareness. He could have started the argument again as if no time had elapsed, the night had made no difference.

He went into the kitchen to wash his face. He gargled noisily, scraped his tongue with his teeth. Then he remembered his toothbrush and toothpaste in his suitcase. As he cleaned his teeth his sister stood watching him. She never used a tooth-brush: they broke a twig and chewed it to clean their mouths.

'You going to go away, *bhai*?' she asked him timidly.

He nodded, with froth in his mouth.

'If you stay, you could teach we what you know,' the girl said.

Romesh washed his mouth and said, '*Baihin*, there are many things I have yet to learn.'

'But what will happen to us?'

'Don't ask me questions, little sister,' he said crossly.

After he had eaten he left the hut and sulked about the village, walking slowly with his hands in his pockets. He wasn't quite sure what he was going to do. He kept telling himself that he would go away and never return, but bonds he had refused to think about surrounded him. The smell of burnt cane was strong on the wind. He went to the pond, where he and Hari used to bath the mules. What to do? His mind was in a turmoil.

Suddenly he turned and went home. He got his cutlass – it was sharp and clean, even though unused for such a long time. Ramlal never allowed any of his tools to get rusty.

He went out into the fields, swinging the cutlass in the air, as if with each stroke he swept a problem away.

Hari said: 'Is time you come. Other people start work long time, we have to work extra to catch up with them.'

There was no friendliness in his voice now.

Romesh said nothing, but he hacked savagely at the canes, and in half an hour he was bathed in sweat and his skin scratched from contact with the cane.

Ramlal came up in the mule cart and called out, 'Work faster! We a whole cartload behind!' Then he saw Romesh and he came down from the cart and walked rapidly across. 'So you come! Is a good thing you make up your mind!'

Romesh wiped his face. 'I am not going to stay, *bap*.' It was funny how the decision came, he hadn't known himself what he was going to do. 'I will help with the crop, you shall get the bonus if I have to work alone in the night. But I am not going to get married. I am going away after the crop.'

'You are mad, you will do as I say.' Ramlal spoke loudly, and other workers in the field stopped to listen.

The decision was so clear in Romesh's mind that he did not say anything more. He swung the cutlass tirelessly at the cane and knew that when the crop was finished, it would be time to leave his family and the village. His mind got that far, and he didn't worry about after that . . .

As the wind whispered in the cane, it carried the news of Romesh's revolt against his parents' wishes, against tradition and custom.

Doolsie, working a short distance away, turned her brown face from the wind. But women and girls working near to her whispered among themselves and laughed. Then one of the bolder women, already married, said, 'Well girl, is a good thing in a way. Some of these men too bad. They does beat their wife too much – look at Dulcie husband, he does be drunk all the time, and she does catch hell with him.'

But Doolsie bundled the canes together and kept silent.

'She too young yet,' another said. 'Look, she breasts not even form yet!'

Doolsie did not have any memories to share with Romesh, and her mind was young enough to bend under any weight.

But the way her friends were laughing made her angry, and in her mind she too revolted against the marriage.

'All-you too stupid!' she said, lifting her head with a child-ish pride so that her sari fell on her shoulder. 'You wouldn't say Romesh is the only boy in the village! And too besides, I wasn't going to married him if he think he too great for me.'

The wind rustled through the cane. Overhead, the sun burned like a furnace.

The Village Washer

SHORTLY AFTER the last war the laundry situation took a turn for the worse in the village of Sans Souci, a sugar-cane hamlet thirty-odd miles from the capital of Port of Spain in Trinidad. Here Ma Lambee ruled supreme as the only washer in the district, and in her sole supremacy she grew careless after she had established herself.

Ma Lambee was old and black and possessed remarkable strength which seemed to bow her legs so she walked like a duck.

With the declaration of war, she began to be neglectful of collars and sleeves and the folds at the bottom of trousers, which places the villagers always looked to judge her workmanship. If a button broke or came off as she scrubbed the clothing with a corn husk, she no longer bothered to mend it, and if a thin shirt ripped as she kneaded her gnarled hands into the cloth, she swore the tear was there before she got the shirt. Was a time when she used four bars of blue soap, and if the dirt and perspiration were still stubborn, bought a bit of washing soda and did her best to get the clothes looking clean again. And was a time when she used four to six buckets of water for one tub of washing: now she used four buckets for two tubs.

Ma Lambee had four flatirons which she heated in a coal pot, wrapping a piece of cloth around the handle to protect her hand as she pressed the clothes. And a good job she did, too, until the war started. Then she bought half the amount of coals and stopped greasing the irons with lard when they were not in use. When she was ironing, she just slid the hot iron around quickly, folded the clothes and put them in the flat, wooden tray, and took them around on her head every Saturday to deliver the laundry.

However, Ma Lambee's excuse that there was a war on didn't stop the villagers from complaining. There were about forty of them living near the canefields where they worked cutting the canes to be transported to the sugar mills two miles away. Of these, about ten did their own washing and the rest depended on Ma Lambee.

But the old woman paid no attention to the complaints. She always promised to do better the following week, but when she came around balancing the tray on her head, customers discovered all the dirt under the collars, and once a merino was so torn that the owner's wife asked her if it was a net to catch fish in the river, and refused to pay for it.

Ma Lambee was unperturbed. In fact, she was 'brazen enough', as a villager put it, to announce that she was raising laundry prices.

'As you know,' she told the women as she stopped at each hut to collect the dirty linen, 'we fighting a war, and the prices of all things going up. So from now on, I will have to charge more to do up the clothes. Long time a shirt was twelve cents. Now it have to be eighteen cents. And long time, skirt was eighteen cents. Now it have to be a shilling.'

From hut to hut, as Ma Lambee passed, words flew furiously.

'Neighbour, you hear about Ma Lambee, how she charging more to do up the clothes now? You can imagine that? And look how careless she getting, not even bothering to sew up a tear, or put back on a button!'

'Yes, is true! I only wish we had another washer in the village; she is the only one, that is why she getting on so!'

'Well, I for one going and try to do the washing myself, if I have time in the evening. The woman must be mad or something!'

'She say the war cause it – what war she talking about?'

A delegation of housewives visited Ma Lambee where she

lived in a broken-down hut under a mango tree, and there was a great argument which lasted for two hours. At the end of that time, the women retreated making threats and shaking their fists at Ma Lambee, who had told them flatly that they could do their own nasty washing if they didn't like her terms.

She lost five customers the following week, but the others were forced to put up with her conditions. Ma Lambee smiled to herself as she went about her washing.

But while she was having her own way word of the villagers' plight reached another hamlet called Donkey City, and another aged negro woman named Ma Procop migrated to Sans Souci with the hope of taking over the business from Ma Lambee.

The day Ma Procop arrived, she was greeted with shouts and smiles, though the people were cautious not to commit themselves too much, fearing she might turn out to be a second Ma Lambee.

But Ma Procop was a clever woman. The first day she put up a notice in the village shop, saying that she was willing to take in laundry at pre-war prices. She said she was an experienced washer from Donkey City and was out to give complete satisfaction to one and all.

It was a long notice, and the spelling was bad and it wasn't worded exactly that way, but the three people in the village who could read saw it and soon everybody knew.

When Ma Lambee heard about it she waddled over to the shop and stuck up a big piece of cardboard on which she had had the village painter write a few words in red paint, stating that she was negotiating with a firm in the city for a new type of washing machine which would make old clothes look like new.

There was no electricity in the village, and it was a lie anyway, but for the first time in her life Ma Lambee was afraid of losing her trade.

That Saturday as she made her rounds she did not get even

a vest to wash. Within a week she had lost all her customers. She was jeered at and the new washing machine became a big joke. Even the children made fun of her, shouting out 'Wash-up washer!' when they saw her.

If Ma Lambee saw Ma Procop walking down the road, she waddled over to the other side and turned her head as if she were smelling something bad. She looked upon the intruder as a hated enemy and thought up means of recovering her trade and at the same time putting Ma Procop to such shame that she would have to go back to Donkey City in a hurry.

At first she tried spreading lies.

'You know,' she told the women she met by the shop, 'that new washer is a nasty woman. She don't even rinse the clothes, and she look so sickly; take care she don't spread disease in the village!'

But Ma Procop's actions soon had the whole village on her side. She even spent a little out of the money she had saved in Donkey City, and worked late in the night sewing on buttons and mending torn clothing. And she made it her business to be friendly, and was especially kind to the children, buying sweets for them and telling them stories.

Ma Lambee now started a malicious rumour that Ma Procop was an obeah woman who changed herself into a blood-sucking animal in the night.

The simple-minded villagers, quick to superstition and belief in omens and evil spirits, became uneasy as the rumour took root.

One night a wounded animal ran into a backyard and left a trail of blood. Next morning Ma Lambee told them:

'Hm, it look like Ma Procop was working overtime last night. I don't know how you people could let that obeah woman live here.'

They began to imagine things. Night noises were attributed to an evil spirit, and though no one pointed directly to Ma

Procop, there was an uneasy air whenever she was around. Quick to see her advantage, Ma Lambee pressed home the fact that the new washer was unusually fond of children – and that little ones were the favourites of obeah women.

She did more than talk. One night she poured a gallon of poison on to the roots of a big silkcotton tree in the centre of the village, and next day divined that as a result of Ma Procop's evil deeds the tree would die before a week passed.

She began to make a study of black magic in order to set the village against Ma Procop. She collected an odd miscellany of liquids and bones and other paraphernalia, and cleared her hut of mirrors and all objects in the sign of the cross.

Things came to a head when the silkcotton tree died. It just withered up, as Ma Lambee had predicted, and within two weeks it was nothing but a standing skeleton.

The village women got together to discuss the situation.

'It happen just as Ma Lambee say, it look like Ma Procop is really a obeah woman.'

'We have to put she to the test – get she to look in a mirror, and make the sign of the cross over she head. If she is really a obeah woman, she can't stand that at all.'

Ma Procop in the meantime was well aware of what was going on in the village. Yet she did nothing, except that one morning she went to Donkey City and came back with a parcel under her arm and a small smile on her lips.

Two days later, on a hot, sunshiny morning, a group of housewives came into Ma Procop's yard as she was hanging out the laundry on some makeshift lines between two mango trees. Ma Lambee was not among them, but while they were foregathering she had been telling them exactly what to do.

'Look in she house – I bet you wouldn't see any mirrors. And I bet you, too, that you find a lot of funny things in the house, like bone and bird feather and bottles and you might even find a skeleton.'

For Ma Lambee had done what she thought would be the last damning thing – she had sneaked into Ma Procop's hut and hidden all the stuff with which she had been practising her own evil acts, and she had removed the only mirror in the room, and a small crucifix near the head of the bed.

Ma Procop hung out a pair of khaki trousers and turned to face the women. They got to the point right away.

'Ma Procop,' the leader said, 'we hear that is you who working obeah in the village and causing evil spirit to walk about in the night.'

'What nonsense you talking?' she put her hands on her hips and looked outraged.

'Well, anyway, we going to search your house.'

They left her standing there and went into the hut. A minute later bottles and bones came hurtling out the window.

'Is true! is true!' the women came tumbling from the hut in fear. 'You really working obeah! Look at all these things we find in your room!'

Ma Procop recovered quickly at this unexpected development.

'All these things you see here,' she waved her hands to the ground, 'they don't belong to me, I swear.' She made the sign of the cross with her two forefingers and kissed it loudly. 'They belong to Ma Lambee. I sure is she who put them in there, because she so spiteful since I come to the village and take away all the washing.'

The women began murmuring among themselves. Then suddenly one of them came forward and shoved a mirror in Ma Procop's face.

With a deliberate calm the washer said, 'Thank you,' and she fixed a piece of coloured cloth she wore on her head, looking straight into the mirror. Then, as if in a rage, she pulled the mirror and dashed it to the ground.

'That is the true test,' one in the group whispered, 'if she really obeah woman she can't look in a mirror. Ma Lambee must be telling lie! It look as if Ma Procop not guilty!'

Ma Procop caught the turning of the tide. 'Listen,' she said. 'Let all of us go over by Ma Lambee and give she the test with a mirror and a cross. I have just what we need hide away inside the house, just give me a chance to get it.'

She dashed inside and came back with the parcel she had brought from Donkey City. She took the lead, heading straight for Ma Lambee's hut.

'You Ma Lambee,' she shouted as they got into the yard, 'you fooling people and saying that is I who working obeah, when is you all the time! Come out here in the yard let we test you!'

Ma Lambee came charging out of the hut. 'What you mean by keeping so much noise in my yard?' she demanded. She tried to keep a steady face but she knew that something had gone wrong.

'Look, we have a mirror and a cross here,' Ma Procop loosened the parcel and stepped ahead of the group. She moved quickly, and turned the mirror full in Ma Lambee's face, at the same time lifting the cross over her head.

No one heard the strange words Ma Procop was fiercely whispering and the weird glint in her eyes, but everyone saw Ma Lambee cower in fear, and a look of extreme terror come into her face. She began to shake, as if she had ague. Then clasping her hands to her head she turned and ran shrieking into the hut.

Ma Procop turned to the frightened villagers.

'Nothing more to worry about,' she said in a tone of authority as she wrapped the mirror and cross into a parcel again. 'You will never have any obeah here as long as I stay in the village.'

The next morning Ma Procop stood by her hut watching Ma Lambee take the road to Donkey City, all her belongings wrapped in a sheet which she had slung over her shoulder.

As the old woman looked back for a last glimpse of Sans

Souci she caught sight of Ma Procop leaning on the fencing, watching her.

With a yell of terror she waddled after her long shadow cast by the morning sun.

Wartime Activities

ONE TIME IN Trinidad during the war one set of thing happen to me, that afterwards I had was to hold my head and bawl. I mean, it going to sound as if I making up the story, but if I lie I die!

We uses to live on a sugar-cane estate name La Romain, and this crop season we was cutting the cane and carting it to the sugar factory. Was a set of Indians living on the estate, and all of we was labourers, sweating in the sun for a few dollars to buy flour and rice in the shop. From the time I was a little fellar I was working on the estate. Never been to school or anything. But don't think I was foolish. I uses to borrow books and magazines from the overseer and study learning. My old man say that is only a waste of time, that I should be bathing the hog-cattle in the pond or fixing the harness on the cart instead of trying to read book, but whenever I had a chance I studying learning.

Well this crop season they put up a bonus for the fellars who could cut the most canes, and I was out in the fields with my cutlass and swiping cane until the sun went down, trying to earn that extra money.

Well I didn't know anything, but the old man and old lady was making plans for me behind my back. Indian parents like to married off their children early, and it look as if the old man was thinking it was time they fix up a married thing for me, in real Indian fashion, which was to make a match with the parents of some girl that I ain't ever see in my life.

The old man went up to Chaguanas that day and come home late in the evening. Chaguanas was a town about twenty-

twenty-five miles from where we was living. And when he come back, he bust the mark.

'*Betah*,' he say, 'I notice these days like you not settle in your mind, I think you coming big man now, and is time you get wife.'

I waiting cool to hear what it is he have on his mind.

'So *betah*,' he go on, 'we make a match for you with a nice girl in Chaguanas. She father have a lot of money and land, so you will get a lot of present at the ceremony.'

'Don't worry with me and that sort of thing,' I say. 'If you think I going married a girl that I ain't even see, you make a mistake.'

'You better don't argue with me,' he say. 'You coming a big man now. You think I didn't see you laying down in the cane with Rookmin daughter last week?'

'I wasn't doing anything,' I say.

'But like you wanted to,' he say. 'Anyway, this thing done settle.'

'This is a modern world,' I say, 'and you can't do thing like that any more.'

'You reading too much book,' he say, and with that he went out to smoke pipe and talk with the neighbours.

I don't know what you would of done in my position, but I know what I did. I didn't talk to him any more about the matter, but when the crop season was over and I get my bonus, bam! I pack up a few things and I out off from the estate and went to San Fernando, which is the brightest town the island have in the south.

This was the first time in my life I ever left the estate, but I didn't want to appear like no country-bookie, so I walking about like I is the heppest man in town. But this time so I frighten to see so much traffic and people moving about, and to hear people talking about the war as if it was going on next door.

I rent a cheap room in Mucurapo Street, which part all the

sports uses to hang out, and I get a job in the oilfields in Point-à-Pierre, about two-three miles away.

It was fine in Mucurapo Street. I get in with the sports and I had to regulate my nights with them. Some of them calling me little boy and force-ripe mango, but all the same I was holding the fort in a big way. One night I just finish seeing a double at the Palace behind the library and I was standing up by the roundabout when a test broach me and say he was bawling, that he come from Port of Spain to see somebody, and now he stranded and can't find no place to sleep. He say that up in town – meaning Port of Spain – he is a hero, but down here he don't know nobody and he don't know if to bounce a sleep on a bench on Harris Promenade or if to go down by the wharf and look for a fishing boat drawn up on the beach.

I ease him up, and let him sleep by me for the night, and next norning he tell me his name was Little One, and that if I ever come up to town I must look him up, though he ain't have a fixed place of abode.

It was about two months after that episode that I get tired with the oilfield work where I was only catching my tail, and I tell the boss to go to hell one morning. They give me a week's wages and tell me to peel off. All the sports in Mucurapo Street sympathise with me, and they want to keep me until things get right, but I was remembering Little One and I had a hankering for the big city.

So I take the midday train and it was crowded for so with all kind of frowsy people. When we reach Port of Spain I get out and start to walk up Frederick Street looking at people. Up here was worse than San Fernando with business and bustling and hustling, and I feel like a fish out of water and I mad to catch the next train back for South.

But while I stand up there thinking who should I see but Little One, doing a window-shop with a sharp piece of skin. As soon as he see me he shout out: 'What you doing here, coolie? Your area is down South.'

So I tell him how things was brown with me and I hear that in town Yankee dollar falling all about.

Little One say: 'You could buy two beers?'

I feel in my pocket and though I don't want to spend no money foolish, I tell him yes. So he give the thing he was with a small walk and we went and sit down and had six beers.

Little One tell me that he could fix up a job for me as a pilot. He say how it have plenty of Yankee and Limey who does come from the ships, and is according to how many of them I could pilot that I would get pay. With that, Little One want to peel off and leave me, but I tell him to hold a key, that it was the first time I ever in Port of Spain, and how I would know where to go and what to do?

'You talking so hep,' Little One say, 'that I thought you born in the town. Go around by Mavis, and she will fix you up. Tell she Little One send you.'

He tell me where to find Mavis, and I went to look for she.

Mavis was living in Charlotte Street, in one of them grim backyard it have there. She was washing clothes in a tub of nasty water in the yard when I reach. I could see the big breasts as she bend to scrub the clothes and I remember the sports in Mucurapo Street and the sun being very hot and everything the first thing I find myself saying is how about a piece.

'Man you damn fast,' Mavis say fiercely, looking up. When she look up it ain't make much difference with the breasts: they pushing out of the bodice as if they on the mark for a race. 'What you mean by coming in my yard in the first place, I mad to call a policeman for you.'

That cool me off and I explain how Little One send me, and Mavis say to go inside and sit down, she coming just now.

Mavis room was a kind of four wall, window, chair-and-table, double-bed affair, with the paint peeling off all about. It remind me of the room I had in San Fernando. It had a coal-pot in a corner and something was cooking.

When Mavis come in I tell she how I was working with Little One, and that he send me round by her to get all the lowdown. Same time I ask she if I could stay until I manage to get a room somewhere. She say she had a man already, that he name Dumboy, that if Little One thought she was some blasted boarder and lodger.

'So how you could hustle if you have a man?' I ask.

'Dumboy have a work with the Yankees in Chaguaramas Bay,' Mavis say, 'and he working nights. Right now he must be loafing round by the market, so you best hads go and come back about six o'clock, else if Dumboy catch you here he beat you like a snake.'

She begin to stir the pot and I smell calaloo.

'How about some food,' I say.

'You best hads go,' Mavis say. 'If Dumboy come he go make big trouble.'

Well the old man don't know what to do, but anyway, I start to breeze around town, then I went in Woodford Square and sit down. Two fellars was arguing about the war, how it look like Germany winning, and how it have so much Yankee in Trinidad now.

I listen to them a little bit, then I went in a café in Duke Street and eat a rock-cake and drink a mauby. Afterwards I went to a 1.30 show at the Empire and they was showing Alan Ladd in *This Gun for Hire*, but after a few reels I was sweating like a horse so I left the theatre and take a tramcar and went for a ride round the savannah.

It was a lovely evening though a bit cloudy and I get out by the Rock Gardens and watch them children and nursemaids and couples making love.

Them nursemaids, they wasn't paying any attention to the children: they only sit down on the grass bad-talking their employers and only now and then one shout out to a child who was playing too near the pond. What happen was a little girl bend down to see if she could see any fish in the pond and she fall in the water. Lucky thing, I was sitting down on a rock near by and I haul the child from the water.

You should hear all them nursemaids.

'The child too stubborn!'

'These white children don't like listen!'

'Good thing the mister was there to haul she out!'

Everybody crowd around and the nursemaid in charge of the child only looking around and saying: 'But what I will tell the madam when we go back?' She take off the wet shoes and socks and dress and spread them out to dry, and she make the child sit down on the grass and lifting her hand threateningly to make the child stop crying.

Well I sizing up the nursemaid, because she don't look so bad at all, and to beat everything she is Indian like me. She have long hair and a coca-cola-bottle figure, and she cursing the child in Hindi, though I is the only one there who know that. I so glad to hear! Right away I start to prattle in Hindi too.

'What your name?' I ask.

'Doolarie,' the thing answer.

'You working for white people?' I ask.

'Yes,' she say. 'They living round by St Clair. I just come to take the child for a walk.'

'Which part you come from?'

'I come from Chaguanas,' she say.

After the children begin to play again we went and sit down under a poui tree and the flowers was falling and she was picking them up and making chain as we talk. She tell me that she run away from home, but when I ask she why she wouldn't say. Then she ask me where I working and I say I have a big job with the Yankees.

The thing looking innocent and pretty and the old man feeling that this is really a sharp craft, and making old-talk and trying to hold her hand, though everytime I do that she pull the hand away.

Doolarie get up to see if the clothes dry, and I sit down

watching her, biting grass and thinking that this was the first time I ever meet a thing that I really fall for, and look at my position!

Doolarie dress the child and stand up by the tram-stop waiting. I ask her what she doing tonight and she say nothing, but the old man can't follow up because he have work to do.

I went on the tram and I pay the fares and tell her I was sorry, but that I working in the night because ships were in, and in a way that was the truth.

'You coming back by the Rock Gardens tomorrow evening?' I ask.

'Yes,' Doolarie say.

'I go try to come,' I say.

She give me a nice smile as I hop off the tram and I feel hearts.

Well that night was very fruitful for Little One and his set-up. I went by Mavis and she give me something to eat, and when it was hunting time the both of we cut out for Park Street. All this time I worrying about Dumboy, if he suspect Mavis and make a tack back from work and find we hustling. And also I remembering Doolarie, and wishing I had a good job and a nice place to live, because I really fall for the thing. I mean, if my father did want me to get married to a thing like Doolarie, I wouldn't mind.

Two Yankee destroyers and a British cruiser was in port that night, so you could imagine what the city like. By Green Corner you couldn't count the limeys, and this time so you only seeing uniform all about the place.

We stop three Yankee and start to talk business but a policeman come up and say to get a move on else he put we up for loitering. Right away Mavis want to fight and curse the policeman, but I hold on to her hand and pull she away, and the Yankees follow up behind. In a little side street we stand up talking and then Mavis hail a taxi and all of we get in it, heading for Barataria, which was a little village where Little One had headquarters, town being too hot for him.

When we get up there we went in a small house off the main road. Like a jam session was going on there. Little One and four-five of his men passing drinks to all kind of uniform. You would think it was a serviceman club. A radio was playing 'They Wouldn't Believe Me' and Little One with a bottle of Vat 19 in his hand, going around and pouring some heavy drink. But I ain't see no girls, and when I ask Mavis she say they in the back room.

After a few minutes the Yankees and the Limeys begin to argue about who should go in the back room first. The Limeys say bloody Yankees and the Yankees say Limey bastards and it look like a big fight was going to start up.

Anyway, Little One hustle in the Yankees first, because a dollar is a dollar, and the Yanks like they was holding big. Then afterwards the Limeys went, but when they come back I could see like they wasn't satisfied, and they went outside in the road and begin to argue with the Yanks.

All this time, the old man feeling uncomfortable, only re-membering the nice piece of skin he see in the gardens, and I can't settle down at all. Little One come up and ask me what happen, but I only shrug my shoulders and turn away.

By the time Mavis was ready to go back to Port of Spain, a big fight start up outside, between America and Britain. It was a one-sided thing, because it had more Yanks than Limeys.

'They taking advantage,' I say.

'You better leave the fight and come go home,' Mavis say.

A Yankee lift up a Limey like he was a child and throw him in the air. When I see that, my blood get hot, and I went in and start to fling wild cuff and kick all about the place. The Yanks must be think that all the local boys coming to fight because all of them stop and begin to pick up hat and cap, and the fight finish right there.

Well I went back home with Mavis, and all this time I only studying Doolarie. Suddenly I want to get out of the city and back to the canefields and the open air and the sun. So that when we was on the bed I just lay there watching up at the cobwebs and scratching. Though Mavis had a busy night like she still wanted to go a rounds, but with Doolarie on my mind I only roll over on the other side and went to sleep.

Next morning I crawl out of bed and put on my clothes. Mavis get up while I was dressing and she thirsty for a rounds, but the old man say no. She get damn vex at that and tell me to get to hell out, that she would put Dumboy on my trail and get him to beat me up.

I went in a Chinese teashop and had a cup of coffee and a ham sandwich.

Sitting down there by a dirty table, I feel as if my whole life toppling down on me, as if I ain't worth anything.

Same time a test come in and ask for a quick coffee, and though nobody ask him why he want it quick, is as if he feel he had to say why, and after saying 'A quick coffee, Ling,' he went on: 'I have to catch a bus, I hear the Americans taking on fellars in Chaguaramas.'

When I hear that, I decide that things so bad with me already that they couldn't be worse, and I catch a bus and went down to the Yankee base.

It had a long line of fellars line up in the gallery of a big building mark Employment Here and I join the line like I knew what it was all about. Pretty soon a Yankee officer come out and look at we as if we is cattle. One by one fellars begins to go in the office, and when it come my turn I walk in brazen.

It had a good-looking sport sitting behind a desk and she hand me a piece of paper and ask me what was my line of work. The first thing that come in my head is mechanic, so I say that. From there I went to another thing who take my fingerprints. Then they send me in another room, where it had fellars with their clothes off, waiting to see the doctor. All of we line up and going up to the doctor one by one, and the doctor sounding the chest and saying, 'O.k., o.k.'

Afterwards they send me to the Mechanic Foreman and he

say twenty bucks a week. 'Look at that engine there,' he say, 'and when the oil gauge drops put in oil and so on.'

Well it had a chair and I sit down, looking at this gauge. That was about half-past ten in the morning. Twelve o'clock come, and the gauge ain't drop. I went in the canteen and buy a hotdog and a packet of Camels and come back.

By the time the siren blow at four o'clock, the gauge ain't fall, and my bottom hot from sitting down and doing sweet f—all.

A fellar come to take over and I ask him about it.

'What you worrying about, old man,' he say, 'you getting the Yankee money to scratch your tail. If the gauge don't fall, it just don't fall. I working here two weeks now and the gauge never fall.'

Back in Port of Spain, I barely had time to catch a tram and go by the Rock Gardens to look and see if Doolarie come to keep the date we make. I went and sit down the same place, on a rock near the pond. Though it have plenty people coming and going, I can't see my thing in the crowd at all. I must be smoke about ten Camels waiting there.

By now it starting to get dark, and I sure she ain't coming, but still I fooling myself that she would come. You see how it is in life? I mean, Doolarie really inspire me to go and look for a decent work and try to make something of myself, and now I was trying and bam! she out off and I can't see her nowhere, I don't even know which part she working, else I could of breezed around by the house and whistle or something.

It didn't have nothing to do but go back to town and lean up on a lamp-post and meditate on life as I eat a piece of water-melon. By and by I went around by Piccadilly to look for a cheap room, and I manage to get one for four dollars a month – that is to tell you what kind of room it was! It had a canvas cot to sleep on, and nothing else at all.

I lay down on the cot thinking hard, but the thoughts wouldn't make no sense. I try to sleep, but a steel band was practising 'Canaan Barrow' by the Dry River and they was making noise like hell.

I get up and went out, walking about with no aim. Near to Royal Theatre it had a donkey-cart with coconut and a Indian fellar opening the nuts with a sharp cutlass. I just start to sport a coconut water – I barely put the nut to my mouth – when I hear a familiar voice and it was shouting: 'That is the man, Dumboy, that is the coolie who force me to sleep with him!'

And before I know what happening in truth, this test Dumboy push the coconut out of my hand and start to beat blows on me, and a crowd gather and start to shout: 'Heave, heave, heave calalay heave!'

Dumboy have on brass knuckles and he only hitting and hitting. I try to grab the coconut from the ground to bust it on his head but when I bend down he raise his knee and it collide with my head and I went tumbling.

I don't know what would of happen there that night if a policeman didn't appear and hold on to me, I think I would of killed Dumboy with blows, even though he was beating me like a snake.

Well I spend the night in a cell, and next morning they take us before the magistrate. Before I have time to say anything the magistrate say: 'I deem you a rogue and a vagabond, thirty dollars or one month's imprisonment.'

Lord, which part I could get thirty dollars from?

'Take him away,' the magistrate say.

I don't know what happen to Dumboy. Mavis was in court and the last thing I hear was she shouting out something to the magistrate. As for me, I find myself in the cell again.

The next day I write my father and tell him to come quick and bring the money with him. When he come, he starting to make all kind of condition, how if he get me out I mustn't run away again, and how I would have to get married. I say yes yes to all that because the only thing I was studying was to get out and get back to where I could feel the wind on my face.

Well a few days after all this my father went up Chaguanas to fix up 'this married thing. When he come back, he look as if he worried.

'What happen?' my mother ask him.

'The girl run away,' he say, 'but they know which part she is, and they going to bring she back home.'

This time so, working in the cane-fields, I forget all about Doolarie, and I did already make up my mind to follow whatever pattern my old man set for me.

About a week later everything ready for the marriage. It have all kind of ceremony in Indian wedding. The parents does offer you all kind of thing, cattle and house and money and so on. But the hurtful part is that the girl you going to married have she face cover up, same as you, and the two of you don't know who the other is. But it had a part of the ceremony where the two of you have to get under a sheet while the priests doing their business, and you should know that when it was time for that, I had a peep at the girl under the sheet.

Doolarie always uses to say, after we did settle down in we own house, that people wouldn't believe when we tell them. But all them things really happen to me while the war was fighting, and if I lie I die.

The Mango Tree

FORTY MILES south of Port of Spain, the town of San Fernando is built picturesquely around a hill, so that the hill itself rises like a giant monument from the centre of the town, and can be seen even from a distance of sixty miles on a clear day. Because of the undulating character of the land, the houses stand on tall posts, and whether you approach the town from the north or south or east – it is bounded by the sea on the west – you climb uphill steeply and then plunge, as it were, into the heart of the town, flashing by canefields that falsely look level with the eye.

About a mile from the sea there is a little mound known as Mount Moriah, and it is a beautiful spot, with the winds from across the green plains always blowing and moving the guava and mango trees, and then sweeping down on the town with the scent of fruit blossoms before it spreads out low and went in gusts across the Gulf of Paria, turning the water into a field of shimmering silver.

Despite the unproductive aspect of the soil – it was brittle in the dry season and clayey in the wet – the few croppers on Mount Moriah managed to earn a living from the unpromising earth. Where the land wasn't cleared for tilling, thick bushes lay luxuriantly, giving the hill the appearance of a heavy green blanket hung out for some sun. The area was owned by an estate proprietor who was surprised when people offered to rent small plots of his wild land. As far as he was concerned, it was enough that some fifty acres were planted with coconut – the rest could lay unfallowed and neglected until that part of the island was being developed, when he hoped to get a good price for his land if the government began to build houses and roads.

Anyone who took the trouble to fight through the bushes had access to the groves of guava and mango that grew wild.

One afternoon a group of boys ran away from school and went to roam in the bushes. They climbed a mango tree and ate the ripe fruit until they couldn't eat any more. Then they began wantonly to pick the mangoes and throw them away, competing to see who could throw the farthest.

One boy stood between a forked branch and hurled a ripe mango with such force that he lost his balance and slipped and fell to the ground. Luckily his fall was broken by a limb below him.

The ripe mango described a turn and a twist as it shot through the air, leaving a descending wake of yellow juice. The boy had thrown skilfully from that difficult position, not up in the air like the others but away from him, and the mango travelled a full eighty yards over bush and bramble before it fell near a cleared piece of land.

This land was tilled by Ma Procop, an old negro woman who lived alone in a hut in the valley. She had a wrinkled face and yellow, spacy teeth. In one of the spaces she gripped a dirty clay pipe firmly with her gums, and she smoked a cheap black tobacco which was grown locally and sold in the village shop.

Ma Procop didn't know anything technical about gardening. She had a plot of land, and things grew in the land, so she just planted the things she wanted. There were clumps of dasheen, a few ochro trees, some eddoes, pepper, sweet potato, sugar cane, and corn. All these were planted without the slightest semblance of order, higgledy-piggledy, as if she had just thrown the different seeds around and hoped for the best.

More to prevent the pilfering of small boys than the ravaging of animals and birds, she had scattered her plot with a weird miscellany of broken bottles, old tin pans, dirty coloured

rags, animal bones, barrel hoops and various constructions of
the sign of the cross. The people in the valley were a superstitious lot, and the scene served to scare away thieves, who
thought the old woman was dealing in obeah. Ma Procop did
what she could to encourage this belief, feeding the rumour
that she was an old hag not right in the head, as she went about
the village selling the produce from her garden.

The mango seed grew unnoticed for six months, then she
discovered it one day while she was reaping corn. The seed
had opened almost on the surface – she could see the thin stem
curled like a green snake in the shell. The four leaves were of
a shining brown colour, drooping in helpless infancy.

Ma Procop raised her hoe, muttering that she didn't want no
mango tree in her garden, but with the blade over her shoulder
she paused and considered. After all, it was only on the border
of the garden, not in the way of her corn. And besides that, it
was possible that the tree was of an uncommon variety.

She bent and looked at the leaves closely. It didn't look like
a long-mango tree, or a dou-dous, or a rose, or a mango-teen,
which grew wild on the hill. Maybe it was a mango-calabash,
or a mango-leatherskin or mango-cheese or mango-spice.

'This is a mango-turpentine tree,' she told herself, thinking
of one of the rarest species of the fruit, 'and when it grow big,
it could sell a penny for one in the market. I think I better
leave it here, it not doing any harm.'

The next day she placed a rusty barrel hoop around the tree,
satisfying a superstitious belief that it would thus thrive better.

Two rainy seasons came and went. The mango tree had won
a valiant battle against the horde of wild bushes and shrubs
which kept encroaching on the border of the garden. Although
it now stood a proud four feet off the ground, there was a kind
of clinging vine which had taken hold of it a year since, twin-
ing round and round the trunk the day it began to take shape
and offer support.

This vine still held on tenaciously, and had thrived with the mango tree, venturing to other branches. Luckily there were no branches on the mango itself; its leaves grew profusedly at the top. The trunk was about twelve inches in circumference at the base, tapering off to six inches.

Ma Procop paid little attention to the tree, she knew it would be years before she reaped any benefit from it.

One morning an Indian woman from the valley left her cow to graze at what she thought was a safe distance from Ma Procop's garden. She had hardly left before the cow, with little effort, tugged the chain away from the small shrub to which it was tied, and went munching through the undergrowth. Finding the young corn in Ma Procop's garden delicious, the animal trampled around, and somehow got the chain wrapped around the mango tree.

Two boys hunting birds came across the cow and one said to the other: 'You know cow does get mad if you show it anything red? Look I have a red handkerchief, let we see what will happen.'

He took the handkerchief from his pocket and dangled it in front of the cow. At first the animal took no notice, it just went on munching at Ma Procop's corn. So the boy came closer, taking courage. Bending his knees preparatory to rapid retreat, he waved the handkerchief right under the cow's nose.

The cow tossed its head in annoyance and made a sudden movement. With a yell of terror the boy turned and ran after his disappearing companion.

The animal, startled by the yell more than anything else, made a tug at the chain to move away. Though the trunk of the mango tree was sturdy, it was still pliable, and that was why it survived. For as the animal tugged the chain strained against the trunk, and for a moment it looked as if the tree was going to break. But it yielded link by link with a chinking sound, and the chain skidded along the trunk as it bent, finally ripping away scores of leaves as it got loose. The mango snapped back into upright position, shaking the bushes around.

When Ma Procop discovered the damage it led to a fierce altercation with the Indian woman, and Ma Procop swore to kill the cow if she ever found it near her garden.

As time went by, a great circular scar appeared on the trunk where the chain had rubbed, and the bark bulged out in an unsightly rugged mark, as if the tree was stricken by some disease.

That dry season no rain fell for weeks, and the earth was parched. It was a time for ground-doves to mate and build their nests in the dry bush, and the boys from the valley to set traps for them.

There was a small quarry on the side of Mount Moriah which faced the sea. The stones here were of a kind of sulphur – when struck together they emitted sparks. Long before the day of the mango tree, in just such a dry season, a bush fire had started, and everyone was convinced that it was because of the sulphur stones.

They were of the same opinion when another bush fire broke out a few days before the dry season was due to end.

It was Ma Procop who set the alarm. She saw smoke and thought someone was burning weeds and rubbish, but after an hour or so the wind was thick with smoke.

She ran down the valley as fast as her creaking limbs were able, waving her hoe in the air and shouting: 'Fire! Fire! Everybody look out for fire!'

Except to ensure that the flames didn't spread to the valley, however, nothing was done to quell the flames. For two days the fire burned slowly, because the wind had abated. Small animals fled the scene and went to the coconut groves near the sea. Luckily for the mango tree the fire was to the lee of the garden. But even so it did not escape altogether. Capricious winds sent an occasional tongue of flame in its direction, and it lost all its leaves, and the trunk was black and charred in places.

Then the wind took strength again – but brought the first

showers of rain for the season, and the threat of the fire was gone.

Three years later a keskidee settled in a fork of the mango tree and built a nest. The tree was now a graceful thing, with four main branches, and showed promise of being fruitful for the next season of mangoes. It had been a hard struggle after the ravages of the fire, but sun and rain had been good. Besides, the fire had razed all the smaller bushes around, and rid the tree of the pestilent vine which had hampered its growth from the very beginning. The tree grew high above the surrounding foliage, alone and away from trees of its kind.

It now afforded a trysting place for a boy and girl from the valley. Most evenings the two of them met under the mango tree, and sat at its roots and leaned against the trunk as they kissed and fondled each other.

One evening, lying on the ground and looking up at the bits of blue sky she could see through the leaves, the girl whimsically challenged the boy to climb the tree.

Taking off his jacket he held on to the lowest branch and hauled himself up, clasping the trunk with his knees for support.

When he was sitting in the fork the girl said, 'I want to come too.'

'If girls climb fruit trees, the fruit will be sour,' the boy said.

'I want to come up,' she pleaded, stretching out her hands to him.

He pulled her up and they sat on the branch.

'This is a nice tree,' she said, but she only said that because she was in love.

And for the same reason, he said, 'It is our tree.'

He took out a penknife and he carved a heart and an arrow, and the girl's initials.

When the mango tree began to flower that season, Ma Procop tied coloured bottles and animal bones to the trunk to scare away thieves. Every day she looked up to see what progress had been made, as if she expected to see flowers one day and ripe mangoes the next.

The weeks went by, and the old woman was anticipating a good crop of fruit. She began at this late stage to concentrate her energies on the mango tree as if she had discovered it for the first time. She weeded the ground around the roots, and she toted buckets of manure from the valley on her head, panting with exertion, and threw it around the tree.

When the flowers had given way to tiny mangoes, almost as small as peas, these fell when the wind was high. Impatient to find out if the mango tree was a rare one, Ma Procop gathered the tiny fruit and took them around to one of her friends in the valley.

'Taste that,' she said, 'tell me what kind of mango it is.'

'It taste just like mango-long to me.'

'Ah, you too foolish, you don't know good mango when you taste one.'

'But how you expect me to know? The mango so small, you can't tell what kind it is by the taste. You have to wait until it get big before you find out.'

So Ma Procop waited through the sun and the rain of June and July and August. And that side of the tree which faced east began to glow with a beautiful shade of pale red as the fruit matured and ripened in the heat of the sun; one side of the mangoes was red, the other side, away from the sun, still green.

And one morning Ma Procop picked up the first ripe mango which had fallen during the night. She held it in her hands and she looked at it, turning it round and round, like a jeweller might examine some rare stone.

'I *know* was mango-turpentine!' she exclaimed triumphantly to herself, sniffing at the fruit, 'and they hard to get now, I should be able to charge a penny for one.'

She was afraid to ask any of the boys in the valley to climb the tree for her, lest they return afterwards to steal. She decided to wait a day or two, then collect those that had fallen to sell.

But she had not reckoned on the attraction the mango tree was, now that it was in fruit which could be seen from a fair distance.

Roaming boys spotted the mangoes and raced each other through the bush. They hesitated when they saw the dangling bones and coloured bottles.

'Obeah,' one of them muttered, 'I not climbing that tree.'

'You too foolish,' another said, 'is only old bones and bottles there.'

But no one made a move to climb the tree.

'Well, why we can't pelt, then?' And the speaker took up a dry branch and tossed it into the midst of a bunch of mangoes.

For two hours, while Ma Procop was doing her shopping in the valley unaware of what was happening, they stoned the tree until there wasn't a ripe mango left.

Still a little afraid of Ma Procop's obeah, they filled their pockets and bosoms and went away to eat far from the scene of the crime. But the first boy to bite one, choosing the ripest and reddest from his collection, spat the skin hastily from his mouth and exclaimed:

'Jeez an' ages! These mango sour for so!'

When Ma Procop saw the ravaged tree next morning she fumed and cursed and stamped around for hours, threatening the world in her wrath and anger.

At length she quietened down and began to see what she could gather.

'I might still be able to make a few cents selling these,' she consoled herself, 'but if I lay hands on those thiefs and them, I will break every bone in they body, so help me God.'

Later, before the sun became too hot, she put the mangoes she had salvaged in a basket and went hawking.

'Mango-turpentine, mango-turpentine!' she called, 'the best for the season, a penny for one!'

After half an hour of this she had walked the length of the village and had no sales. She reduced the price.

'Mango-turpentine, mango-turpentine! the best for the season, only a cent for one!'

Out of two dozen she managed to sell twenty. She was returning home with the other four when she met a boy and girl holding hands, walking down the village road.

'Buy a sweet mango for your girl-friend, mister,' she called out, 'sweet mango-turpentine, only a cent for one, only four remaining.'

The boy bought the mangoes and Ma Procop thanked him and went into the shop to buy a little tobacco for her pipe.

The boy wiped one of the mangoes on his trousers and gave it to the girl. As soon as she had bitten the fruit she spat the juice out.

'Man, this mango sour like anything!' She grimaced and threw it far from her.

The boy bit his and went through the same motions, screwing up his face. 'Yes, they really sour. Nobody could eat these. You know what, I bet you a girl climb that mango tree, that is why they so sour!'

The next time she went into her garden Ma Procop looked up mournfully at the mango tree.

'Everybody eat from you,' she said, 'the boys thief from you and they eat, and I sell what I could and other people eat. But is my mango tree, and up to now I ain't taste one of these nice mangoes yet!'

She began to hoe a spot for corn. 'Anyway,' she straightened her back and addressed the tree again, 'I hope next year please God you bear more, all that manure I waste on you, and you only bear one set of mango and stop.'

She thought about the matter as she hoed the weeds, jabbing at the earth as if she was striking the tree itself. She thought herself into a great rage against the tree, so that she stopped hoeing and eyed it balefully.

Then she took two quick steps and began hacking away at the mango tree with her hoe, until she fell back panting.

A breeze blew and the leaves rustled and the branches of the mango tree swayed, and the stem of a lonely mango, hidden by the green leaves, broke and the fruit fell with a thud at Ma Procop's feet.

For a moment she looked at it vacantly. Then she bent and picked it up.

It was the rosiest mango. It had grown full and big, attaining a shiny red colour. It seemed to be bursting with juice, and after a feeling of disbelief Ma Procop's mouth watered as she thought how sweet it must be, especially as it was surely the last one the tree would yield for that season.

Sitting and leaning against the trunk of the mango tree to rest a little and the better to enjoy the fruit, she wiped it carefully with her hands and sunk her teeth into the skin.

Gussy and the Boss

THE ORGANISATION known as Industrial Corporation was taken over shortly after the war by a group of European businessmen with interests in the West Indies, and renamed the New Enterprises Company, with a financial backing of £50,000. The new owners had the buildings renovated where they stood on the southern outskirts of Port of Spain, a short distance from the railway station.

While the buildings were being painted and the old office furniture replaced, none of the employees knew that the company had changed hands. They commented that it was high time the dilapidated offices were given a complete overhauling and they tried out the new chairs and desks and came to words over who should have the mahogany table and this cabinet and that typewriter.

When the buildings had a new face and they were just settling down with renewed ambitions and resolutions to keep the rooms as tidy as possible, Mr Jones, the boss, called a staff meeting one evening and told them.

He said he was sorry he couldn't tell them before – some arrangement with the new owners – but that Industrial Corporation was going out of business. He said he had been hoping that at least part of the staff would be able to remain, but he was sorry, the matter was entirely out of his hands, and they all had to go.

There were ten natives working in the offices at the time, and there was a middle-aged caretaker called Gussy. Gussy had one leg. A shark had bitten off the other in the Gulf of Paria while he was out fishing with some friends.

The ten employees – four girl typists and six clerks – had never thought of joining a trade union, partly because they felt that trade unions were for the poor struggling labourers and they were not of that class, and partly because the thought had never entered their heads that such a situation might arise. As it was, they could do nothing but make vain threats and grumble; one chap went to a newspaper and told the editor the whole story and asked him to do something about it. The editor promised and next day a reporter interviewed Mr Jones, and the following morning a small news item appeared saying that Industrial Corporation had been taken over by a group of wealthy Europeans, and that there was no doubt that the colony would benefit as a result. because new industries would be opened.

After two weeks the ten workers had cleared out leaving only Mr Jones and Gussy. Gussy gathered his courage and spoke to Mr Jones.

He said: 'Boss, you know how long I here with the business. I is a poor man, boss, and I have a ailing mother to support, and I sure I can't get a work no where else. Please chief, you can't talk to the new bosses and them, and put·in a good word for this poor one-legged man, and ask them to keep me? I ain't have a big work, is just to stay in the back of the place and see that nobody interfere with anything. Make a try for me please, pusher, the Good Lord will reward you in due course, and I would appreciate it very much.'

Mr Jones heard Gussy mumble through this long speech and he promised to see what he could do, grateful that the care-taker had given him the opportunity to make peace in his own mind, thinking that Gussy's salvation would absolve him from responsibility for the sacking of the others.

A week later the new staff arrived. Gussy hid behind a door in the storeroom and peeped between a crack be-cause he was afraid to face all the new people at once. His agitation increased greatly as he saw that they were all white people. Were they all bosses then? The women too?

Later in the morning, while he was sweeping out the storeroom as noiselessly as possible, one of the new employees came to him.

'You're Gussy, the caretaker?' he asked in a kind voice.

Gussy dropped the broom and shoved his crutch under his arm quickly, standing up like a soldier at attention.

'Yes boss, I is the caretaker.'

'Mr Blade would like a word with you. He is the new manager, as you probably know.'

'What about, sir? My job is the caretaker job. My name is Gussy. I lives in Belmont. Age forty-five. No children. I lives with my mother. I gets pay every Friday . . .'

'I know all that,' the young man smiled a little. 'I am in charge of the staff we have here now. But Mr Blade wants to see you. Just for a little chat, he likes to be personally acquainted with everyone who works for him.'

Gussy's eyes opened wide and showed white. 'So I still have the job, chief? You all not going to fire me?'

'Of course not! Come along, Mr Blade is a busy man.'

When he returned to his post at the back of the building a few minutes later Gussy was full of praise for the new boss, mumbling to himself because there was no one to talk with. When he went home in the evening he told his mother:

'You can't imagine! He is a nice man, he even nicer than Mr Jones! He tell me is all right, that I could stay on the job as the caretaker, being as I was here so long already. When I tell you the man nice!'

But as the days went by Gussy wasn't happy at his job anymore. He couldn't get accustomed to the idea that white people were working all around him. He treated every one as he treated Mr Blade, stumping along as swiftly as he could to open the garage door or fill the water cooler or do whatever odd chore he was called upon to perform. In the old days he was in the habit of popping in and out of the outer office, sharing a word here and a joke there with the native workers. But now, he kept strictly to the back of the building, turning out an hour earlier to clean out the offices before any of the staff arrived. True, they treated him friendly, but Gussy couldn't get rid of the idea that they were all bosses.

After a week of loneliness he ventured near to the office door and peeped inside to see how the white people were working.

The young man who had spoken to him the first day, Mr Garry, saw him and called him inside.

Gussy stumped over to his desk with excuses.

'I was only looking to see if everything all right, boss, to see if anybody want anything, the weather hot, I could go and get some ice outside for you right now . . .'

Garry said: 'It's all right, Gussy, and I don't mind you coming to the office now and then.' He lowered his voice. 'But you watch out for the boss's wife. Sometimes she drops in unexpectedly to see him, and it wouldn't do for her to see you out here, because . . . well, because here is not the place you're supposed to be, you understand?'

'But sure boss, Mr Garry, I won't come back here again, not at all at all unless you send for me, I promise you that boss, sure, sure . . .

Whenever Mr Blade drove up in his Buick Eight, Gussy was there with a rag to wipe the car.

'You know, Gussy,' Mr Blade told him one morning, 'you manage to do more with that one leg of yours than many a normal man I know.'

'Thank you very much respectfully and gratefully, boss sir, all the offices clean, the water cooler full up, all the ink pots full up, the storeroom pack away just as Mr Garry want it . . .'

One evening when he had opened the garage door for the boss and he was reversing out – with Gussy standing at the back and giving all sorts of superfluous directions with his crutch which Mr Blade ignored – the boss looked out of the car window and said:

'By the way, Gussy, how much do you work for?'

'Ten dollars a week chief sir, respectfully, it not very much, with me minding my poor mother, but is enough, sir, I can even manage on less than that if you feel that it too much . . .'

'I was thinking of giving you more, what with the rising cost of living. Let me see, today is Wednesday. Come to see me on Friday morning and we'll talk about it.'

Mr Blade drove off with Gussy's effusive thanks just warming up.

The next afternoon was hot, and Gussy was feeling drowsy as he sat on a soapbox in the storeroom. He felt a strong temptation to go and stand near the office door. The knowledge that he was soon going to earn a bigger salary gave him courage. He got up and went and positioned himself just outside the door.

He was just in time to hear Mr Garry telling the others about how his plane was shot down during the war, and Gussy listened wide-eyed.

Gussy heard a step behind him and turned around. He didn't know it was the boss's wife, but it wouldn't have made any difference, he would have behaved the same way with any white person.

'Just looking in to see if the bosses and them want anything at all no offence madam indeed . . .'

This time he dropped the crutch in his consternation.

The woman gave him a withering look and swept past the outer office.

Mr Blade was sitting in his swivel chair, facing the sea. It was a hot afternoon and he had the window fully opened, but the wind that came in was heavy and lifeless, as if the heat had taken all the spirit out of it.

Mr Blade was a kindly man newly arrived in the colony from England. He was also a weak man, and he knew it. Sometimes Blade was afraid of life because he was weak and couldn't make decisions or face up to facts and circumstances.

The palms of his hands were always wet when he was excited or couldn't find the answer to a problem.

As he sat and watched the sea sparkle, he was thinking in a general sort of way about his life, and when his wife burst into the office he started.

'Oh hello, dear, didn't expect to see you today.'

Whenever Blade looked at his wife he saw the symbol of his weakness. All his faults were magnified and concentrated on her face, which was like a mirror in which he looked and shrank.

'Herbert.' She also had a most disquieting habit of getting to the point right away. 'I thought you had dismissed all the natives who were here before we came?'

'Of course, dear. As you can see, we only have Europeans and one or two whites who were born in the island.'

'I met a dirty one-legged man outside the office just as I was coming in – who's he?'

'Oh heavens, he's only the caretaker! Surely you didn't think he was on the staff?' Blade shifted his eyes and looked at an almanac on the wall above his wife's head.

'You'll have to get rid of him, you know.'

When she finished speaking, he knew that those last words would stay long after she left, from the tone in which she spoke. All their conversations were like that – everything else forgotten but the few words she spoke in that tone. He had gotten into the habit of listening for it. She had a special way of summing up, of finalising matters. He knew, from that moment – in a quick panic of fear which brought the sweat out on his palms – that the caretaker would have to go.

'Let's don't argue about it now, dear. I don't feel very well in this damned heat.'

And the next morning Blade sat down in the swivel chair and he faced the sea again. He knew he was going to fire Gussy, but he tried to think that he wasn't. He wiped the palms of his hands with a white handkerchief. All his life it had been like that; he felt the old fear of uncertainty and instability which had driven him from England return, and he licked his lips nervously.

He swung the chair and looked at the almanac on the wall. He addressed it as if it were his wife.

'That's a silly attitude to adopt,' he said to the almanac in a firm voice. 'You can't do that sort of thing. On the contrary, it is a good prestige for the place that we have a coloured worker. I think we should have more – after all, they do the work just as well.'

He sneered at the almanac, then looked for some other object in the room to represent Gussy. He fixed his eyes on the out-basket on his desk.

'The way how things are at present,' he told the basket, 'I'm afraid you'll have to go. We don't really need a caretaker any more, and we can always get a woman to come in and clean the offices. I personally didn't have anything to do with it, mind you, it was . . . er, the decision of the directors. I am sorry to lose you, Gussy, you are a hard, honest worker.'

For a minute Blade wondered if there wasn't something he could do – post money secretly to the man every week, or maybe give him a tidy sum to tide him over for a few months.

The next minute he was laughing mirthlessly – once the handkerchief fell and he unconsciously rubbed his hands together and he heard the squelching sound made by the perspiration. And he talked and reasoned with all the objects in the room, as if they were companions, and some objects agreed and others didn't.

The pencil and the inkpot said it was all right, he was a fool to worry, why didn't he get Garry to do the dirty work, and the almanac told him to get it over with quickly for Christ's sake, but the window and the wall and the telephone said Gussy was a poor, harmless creature and he Blade was a spineless, unprincipled dog, who didn't know his own mind and wasn't fit to live.

With an impatient, indecisive gesture Blade jabbed the button on his desk. One of the girls opened the door.

'That caretaker we have – what is his name – Gusher or Gully or something like that' – the lie in his deliberate lapse of memory stabbed him – 'send him in to see me, will you, please.'

Gussy was waiting to be called. He had told Mr Garry how the boss would be wanting to see him, and that was why he was keeping so near to the office, so they wouldn't have any trouble finding him.

Gussy didn't have any idea how much more money he was going to get, but whatever it was, first thing he was going to do was buy a bottle of polish and shine down the boss's car to surprise him. After that, anything could happen.

He stood in a corner, quietly calculating on his fingers how much he would have to pay if he wanted to put down three months' rent in advance.

'Oh, there you are, Gussy,' the girl caught sight of him as she came out. 'Mr Blade wants to see you. You'd better go in right away.'

'Thank you madam, I am right here, going in to see the boss right away, with all due respects, no delay at all.'

Gussy shoved his crutch under his armpit and stumped as softly as he could to the boss's door.

A Drink of Water

THE TIME WHEN the rains didn't come for three months and the sun was a yellow furnace in the sky was known as the Great Drought in Trinidad. It happened when everyone was expecting the sky to burst open with rain to fill the dry streams and water the parched earth.

But each day was the same; the sun rose early in a blue sky, and all day long the farmers lifted their eyes, wondering what had happened to Parjanya, the rain god. They rested on their hoes and forks and wrung perspiration from their clothes, seeing no hope in labour, terrified by the thought that if no rain fell soon they would lose their crops and livestock and face starvation and death.

In the tiny village of Las Lomas, out in his vegetable garden, Manko licked dry lips and passed a wet sleeve over his dripping face. Somewhere in the field a cow mooed mournfully, sniffing around for a bit of green in the cracked earth. The field was a desolation of drought. The trees were naked and barks peeled off trunks as if they were diseased. When the wind blew, it was heavy and unrelieving, as if the heat had taken all the spirit out of it. But Manko still opened his shirt and turned his chest to it when it passed.

He was a big man, grown brown and burnt from years of working on the land. His arms were bent and he had a crouching position even when he stood upright. When he laughed he showed more tobacco stain than teeth.

But Manko had not laughed for a long time. Bush fires had swept Las Lomas and left the garden plots charred and smoking. Cattle were dropping dead in the heat. There was scarcely any water in the village; the river was dry with scummy mud. But with patience one could collect a bucket of water. Boiled, with a little sugar to make it drinkable, it had to do.

Sometimes, when the children knew that someone had gone to the river for water, they hung about in the village main road waiting with bottles and calabash shells, and they fell upon the water-carrier as soon as he hove in sight.

'Boil the water first before drinking!' was the warning cry. But even so two children were dead and many more were on the sick list, their parents too poor to seek medical aid in the city twenty miles away.

Manko sat in the shade of a mango tree and tried to look on the bright side of things. Such a dry season meant that the land would be good for corn seeds when the rains came. He and his wife Rannie had been working hard and saving money with the hope of sending Sunny, their son, to college in the city.

Rannie told Manko: 'We poor, and we ain't have no education, but is all right, we go get old soon and dead, and what we have to think about is the boy. We must let him have plenty learning and come a big man in Trinidad.'

And Manko, proud of his son, used to boast in the evening, when the villagers got together to talk and smoke, that one day Sunny would be a lawyer or a doctor.

But optimism was difficult now. His livestock was dying out, and the market was glutted with yams. He had a great pile in the yard which he could not sell.

Manko took a look at his plot of land and shook his head. There was no sense in working any more today. He took his cutlass and hoe and calabash shell which had a string so he could hold it dangling. He shook it, and realised with burning in his throat that it was empty, though he had left a few mouthfuls in it. He was a fool; he should have known that the heat would dry it up if he took it out in the garden with him. He licked his lips and, shouldering the tools, walked slowly down the winding path which led to his hut.

Rannie was cooking in the open fireplace in the yard. Sunny was sitting under the poui tree, but when he saw his father he ran towards him and held the calabash shell eagerly. Always when Manko returned from the fields he brought back a little water for his son. But this time he could only shake his head.

'Who went for water today by the river?' he asked Rannie.

'I think was Jagroop,' she answered, stirring the pot with a large wooden spoon, 'but he ain't coming back till late.'

She covered the pot and turned to him. 'Tomorrow we going to make offering for rain,' she said.

Next day, Las Lomas held a big feast, and prayers were said to the rain god, Parjanya. And then two days later, a man called Rampersad struck water in a well he had been digging for weeks. It was the miracle they had been praying for. That day everyone drank their fill, and Rampersad allowed each villager a bucket of water, and Manko told Sunny: 'See how blessing doesn't only come from up in the sky, it does come from the earth, too.'

Rampersad's wife was a selfish and crafty woman, and while the villagers were filling their buckets she stood by the doorway of their hut and watched them. That night she told her husband he was a fool to let them have the water for nothing.

'They have money hide up,' she urged him. 'They could well pay for it. The best thing to do is to put barb' wire all round the well, and set a watchdog to keep guard in the night so nobody thief the water. Then say you too poor to give away for nothing. Charge a dollar for a bucket and two shillings for half-bucket. We make plenty money and come rich.'

When Rampersad announced this, the villagers were silent and aghast that a man could think of such a scheme when the whole village was burning away in the drought, and two children had died.

Rampersad bought a shotgun and said he would shoot anyone he found trespassing on his property. He put up the barbed wire and left a ferocious watchdog near the well at nights.

As April went, there was still no sign in the sky. In Las Lomas, the villagers exhausted their savings in buying Rampersad's water to keep alive.

Manko got up one morning and looked in the tin under his bed in which he kept his money. There was enough for just two buckets of water. He said to Rannie: 'How long could you make two buckets of water last, if we use it only for drinking?'

'That is all the money remaining?' Rannie looked at him with fear.

He nodded and looked outside where the poui tree had begun to blossom. 'Is a long time now,' he said softly, 'a long time, too long. It can't last. The rain will fall, just don't be impatient.'

Rannie was not impatient, but thirst made her careless. It happened soon after the two buckets were empty. She forgot to boil a pan of river water, and only after she had drunk a cupful did she realise her fatal mistake. She was afraid to tell Manko; she kept silent about the incident.

Next day, she could not get out of bed. She rolled and tossed as fever ravaged her body.

Manko's eyes were wide with fright when he saw the signs of fever. Sunny, who had not been to school for weeks, wanted to do whatever he could, anything at all, to get his mother well so she could talk and laugh and cook again.

He spoke to his father after Rannie had fallen into a fitful sleep, with perspiration soaking through the thin white sheet.

'No money remaining for water, *bap*?'

Manko shook his head.

'And no money for doctor or medicine?'

He shook his head again.

'But how it is this man Rampersad have so much water and we ain't have any? Why don't we just go and take it?'

'The water belong to Rampersad,' Manko said. 'Is his own, and if he choose to sell it, is his business. We can't just go and take, that would be thiefing. You must never thief from another man, Sunny. That is a big, big, sin. No matter what happen.

'But is not a fair thing,' the boy protested, digging his hands into the brittle soil. 'If we had clean water, we could get *mai* better, not so?'

'Yes, *beta*,' Manko sighed and rose to his feet. 'You stay and mind *mai*, I going to try and get some river water.'

All day, Sunny sat in the hut brooding over the matter, trying hard to understand why his mother should die from lack of water when a well was filled in another man's yard.

It was late in the evening when Manko returned. As he had expected, the river was nearly dry, a foul trickle of mud not worth drinking. He found the boy quiet and moody. After a while, Sunny went out.

Manko was glad to be alone. He didn't want Sunny to see him leaving the hut later in the night, with the bucket and the rope. It would be difficult to explain that he was stealing Rampersad's water only because it was a matter of life or death.

He waited impatiently for Rannie to fall asleep. It seemed she would never close her eyes. She just turned and twisted restlessly, and once she looked at him and asked if rain had fallen, and he put his rough hand on her hot forehead and said softly no, but that he had seen a sign that evening, a great black cloud low down in the east.

Then suddenly her fever rose again, and she was delirious. This time he could not understand what she said. She was moaning in a queer, strangled way.

It was midnight before she fell into a kind of swoon, a red flush on her face. Manko knew what he must do now. He stood looking at her, torn between the fear of leaving her and the desperate plan that he had made. She might die while he was gone, and yet – he must try it.

He frowned as he went out and saw the moon like a night

sun in the sky, lighting up the village. He turned to the east and his heart leapt as he saw the cloud moving towards the village in a slow breeze. It seemed so far away, and it was moving as if it would take days to get over the fields. Perhaps it would; perhaps it would change direction and go scudding down into the west, and not a drop of water.

He moved off towards the well, keeping behind the huts and deep into the trees. It took him ten minutes to get near the barbed wire fence, and he stood in the shadow of a giant silk-cotton tree. He leaned against the trunk and drew in his breath sharply as his eyes discerned a figure on the other side of the well, outside the barbed wire.

The figure stopped, as though listening, then began clambering over the fence.

Even as he peered to see if he could recognise who it was, a sudden darkness fell as the cloud swept over the moon in the freshening wind.

Manko cast his eyes upwards swiftly, and when he looked down again the figure was on the brink of the well, away from the sleeping watchdog.

It was a great risk to take; it was the risk Manko himself had to take. But this intrusion upset his plan. He could not call out; the slightest sound would wake the dog, and what it did not do to the thief, Rampersad would do with his shotgun.

For a moment, Manko's heart failed him. He smelt death very near – for the unknown figure at the well, and for himself, too. He had been a fool to come. Then a new frenzy seized him. He remembered the cruel red flush on Rannie's cheeks when he had left her. Let her die happy, if a drop of water could make her so. Let her live, if a drop of water could save her. His own thirst flared in his throat; how much more she must be suffering!

He saw the bucket slide noiselessly down and the rope paid out. Just what he had planned to do. Now draw it up, cautiously, yes, and put it to rest gently on the ground. Now kneel and take a drink, and put the fire out in your body. For God's sake, why didn't the man take a drink? What was he waiting for? Ah, that was it, but be careful, do not make the slightest noise, or everything will be ruined. Bend your head down . . .

Moonrays shot through a break in the cloud and lit up the scene.

It was Sunny.

'*Beta!*' Before he could think, the startled cry had left Manko's lips.

The dog sprang up at the sound and moved with uncanny swiftness. Before Sunny could turn, it had sprung across the well, straight at the boy's throat.

Manko scrambled over the fence, ripping away his clothes and drawing blood. He ran and cleared the well in a great jump, and tried to tear the beast away from the struggling boy. The dog turned, growling low in the throat as it faced this new attacker.

Manko stumbled and fell, breathing heavily. He felt teeth sink into his shoulder and he bit his lip hard to keep from screaming in pain.

Suddenly the dog was wrenched away as Sunny joined the fight. The boy put his arms around the dog's neck and jerked it away from his father with such force that when the animal let go they both fell rolling to the ground.

Manko flung out his arm as he sprang up. In doing so, he capsized the bucket of water with a loud clang. Even in the struggle for life he could not bear to see the earth sucking up the water like a sponge. In fear and fury, he snatched the empty bucket and brought it down with all his strength on the dog's head.

The animal gave a whimper and rolled off the boy and lay still.

'Who that, thiefing my water?' Rampersad came running out into the yard, firing his shotgun wildly in the air.

'Quick, boy! Over the fence!' Manko grabbed the bucket and tossed it over. He almost threw Sunny to safety as the boy faltered on the wire. Then he half-dragged his own bleeding body up, and fell exhausted on the other side.

Sunny put his arm under his father and helped him up. Together they ran into the shadow of the trees.

The noise of the gun and Rampersad's yells had wakened the whole village, and everyone was astir.

Father and son hid the bucket in a clump of dry bush and, waiting for a minute to recover themselves, joined the crowd which was gathering in front of Rampersad's hut.

Rampersad was beside himself with rage. He threatened them all with jail, screaming that he would find out who had stolen the water and killed the dog.

'Who is the thief? You catch him?' The crowd jeered and booed. 'It damn good. Serve you right.' Clutching his father's arm tightly, Sunny danced and chuckled with delight at Rampersad's discomfiture.

But suddenly silence and darkness fell together. A large black blob of cloud blotted out the moon. The sky was thick with clouds piling up on each other and there was a new coolness in the wind.

As one, the crowd knelt and prayed to the rain god. The sky grew black; it looked as if the moon had never been there. For hours they prayed, until Manko, thinking of Rannie, gently tapped his son and beckoned him away. They walked home hand in hand.

It was Sunny who felt the first drop. It lay on his hand like a diamond shining in the dark.

'*Bap?*' He raised questioning eyes to his father. 'Look!'

As Manko looked up, another drop fell on his face and rolled down his cheek. The wind became stronger; there was a swift fall of some heavy drops. Then the wind died like a sigh. A low rumble in the east; then silence. Perhaps Parjanya was having a joke with them, perhaps there would be no rain after all.

And then it came sweeping in from the north-east, with a rising wind. Not very heavy at first, but in thrusts, coming and going. They opened their mouths and laughed, and water fell in. They shouted and cried and laughed again.

Manko approached the hut where Rannie lay, and he was trembling at what he would find. He said to the boy: '*Beta*. You stay here. I go in first to see *mai*.' The boy's face went rigid with sudden fear. Though he was already drenched to the skin, he took shelter under the poui tree in the yard.

Manko was hardly inside the door when he gave a sharp cry of alarm. He thought he saw a ghostly figure tottering towards him, its face luminous-grey. He flattened himself against the wall and closed his eyes. It was cruel of the gods to torment him like this. This was not Rannie: Rannie was lying in bed in the next room, she could not be alive any more.

'Manko.' It was her voice, and yet it was not her voice. 'What noise is that I hear? Is rain?'

He could not speak. Slowly, he forced himself to stretch out his hand and touch her forehead. It felt cold and unnatural.

He withdrew his hand, and began to tremble uncontrollably.

'Manko,' the lips formed the words. 'Manko, give me water!'

Something fell to the floor with a clatter. He saw that it was a tin cup, and that she had been holding it in her hand. She swayed towards him, and he caught her. Then Manko knew that it was a miracle. Rannie was shaking with cold and weakness, but the fever was gone, and she was alive.

Realisation burst upon him with such force that he almost fainted.

He muttered: 'I will get some for you.'

He picked up the cup and ran out into the lashing rain. Sunny, watching from the poui tree, was astonished to see his father standing motionless in the downpour. He had taken off his shirt, and his bare back and chest were shining with water.

His face, uplifted to the sky, was the face of a man half-crazy with joy. He might be laughing or crying, Sunny could not tell; and his cheeks were streaming, perhaps with tears, perhaps with Parjanya's rain.

Calypso in London

ONE WINTER a kind of blight fall on Mangohead in London. As if he can't make a note nohow, no matter where he turn. Not only he can't get a work nowhere, but he can't even pick up a little thing to keep company with, nor bounce a borrow from any of the boys, nor even get a pleasant good morning from the landlady.

Mangohead sit down in his room to ponder on the situation. Mangohead come from St Vincent, and if you don't know where that is that is your hard luck. But I will give you a clue – he uses to work on a arrowroot plantation. Now I suppose you want to know what arrowroot is, eh?

Mangohead had a sharp work in the summer. You ever notice sometimes, when you hustling to the office, that it have four-five fellars stand up or sit down around a hole in the pavement, and one fellar inside the hole as if he fixing some kind of electric cable, with half a cigarette in his mouth? Well Mangohead had a work, where he was one of the four-five fellars who sitting around.

Things was all right until it start to get cold. They was digging up the road in Hampstead to lay cable, and it was so cold poor Mangohead was shivering. And them other English fellars giving him tone, asking him if he wouldn't like to be in the tropics right now, and saying: 'Too cold for you mate?' and winking and nudging one another when Mangohead stand up near the wood fire that they light on the pavement to keep warm.

Well Mangohead try hard with the work, bearing the cold. Then one frosty morning when he was digging, he lift up a spadeful of dirt to throw up on the bank, and when he throw his hands over his shoulder, as if his hands catch cramp and couldn't come back. Mangohead hands stay like that, as if they get frozen in that position, and all he try he couldn't move his hands. At last, by turning his body a little, he manage to get the hands a little lower, and he drop the spade.

Mangohead climb up out of the trench, went and wash his hands, and tell the foreman that he finish with the work.

He thought it would of been easy to get another work, somewhere out of the cold. But the blight start from the day he leave the trench.

Mangohead comb all the factories and canteens, and he ask the boys about vacancies, but nothing was doing.

One morning he get a wire that a cigarette factory in the East End was taking fellars, and he hustle and went, but when he get there the fellar say sorry, no vacancies. This time so, I don't have to tell you how the winter grim in London – I mean, I don't think it have any other place in the world where the weather so powerful, and Mangohead drifting through the fog and the smog and snow getting in his shoes and the wind passing right through him as if he ain't have on any clothes at all.

Well Mango had a friend in the East End, name Hotboy, who was a fellar from Trinidad what used to compose calypso. Hotboy have a mysterious way of living. All day long he sitting in a Indian tailor shop in Cable street, talking politics, or else harking back to the old days in Trinidad, because the Indian fellar who own the shop name Rahamut and he also come from Trinidad. Sometimes Hotboy in some real oldtalk about them days back home, telling Rahamut about how he was one of the best calyposonians it had in Trinidad, how the compose numbers like 'I Saw You Doing It Last Night' and 'That Is A Thing I Could Do Anytime, Anywhere'. Well Hotboy always saying about how he would make a comeback one day, how he would compose a calypso that would be hearts, and it would sell plenty and he would make money and come rich.

All these things Mangohead remember when he get turn away from the cigarette factory, and he start to make a bee for the tailor shop, hoping to make a little borrow from Hotboy, something like ten shillings, or if not, five, or if not, a two and six, or if not at least a cuppa, old man. Also, Mangohead suddenly feeling creative. As if all the troubles he in put him in a thoughtful mood, and while he meditating on the downs of life, he feel like composing a calypso that would tell everybody how life treating him.

> It had a time in this country
> When everybody happy excepting me
> I can't get a work no matter how I try
> It look as if hard times riding me high.

This was not the first time Mangohead get vap to create calypso: many times before Hotboy drive him away when he go to him with some sharp ideas, but Mangohead feel that this is it, that this time he really have something, that Hotboy sure to like the words and set up a tune for them.

When he get to the tailor shop, Hotboy in a hot debate with Rahamut about the Suez issue. 'If I was Nasser . . .' Hot was saying, and going on to say what and what he wouldn't do.

Now, from the time Hot see Mango, he stop talking about the Suez Canal, and before poor Mango could say anything Hot say:

'Yes, I know what you come round here for, since you borrow ten shillings from me last week you lose the address, and you only come now to tell me that you expecting a work next week, and if I could lend you another ten please God until you start to work. But Mangohead you lie, you hear? I telling you in front, no, no, no. I ain't lending you a nail till you pay me back that ten.'

'But look at my crosses!' Mango rise to the occasion fast. '*Me* borrow money from you! That was the last thing in my mind! You so bad-minded you can't feel that I just come to pay a social visit?'

But Hot cagey, he only grunting and eyeing Mango suspiciously, as if he still expect Mango to plead for a borrow.

Mango say: 'Hotboy, I have an idea here for a calypso that is hearts. I sure when you hear it you will agree, and set up a tune for it. We might even get it play by the BBC.'

Now Hot tired asking the Mango to leave calypso alone, telling him that that is not his line. Time and again he chase Mango when Mango come with some stupid words, saying that the words would make a firstclass calypso.

'But Mango, who tell you you could write calypso? When you was in Trinidad you only used to work drilling oil in Point-à-Pierre. How much time I have to tell you to leave calypso alone?'

'But man Hotboy, I sure this time! I have some words here that would kill people when they hear.'

Hotboy get up off the cardboard carton he was sitting on: same time Rahamut see the carton break up how Hotboy was sitting on it and he say: 'Look what the hell you do with the box, I tell you not to sit down on it.'

But Hotboy ignore him, and turn to Mango again: 'You sure you don't want to borrow money?'

Mango make the sign of the cross with his forefingers and kiss it.

'All right,' Hotboy say grudgingly, 'let we go in the back of the shop.'

So they went in the back of the shop, which part Rahamut have a table and two chairs, and they sit down there and Hotboy tell Mango: 'Let me hear these brave words.'

So Mango begin, but from the time he begin Hotboy chock his ears with his fingers and bawl out: 'Lord old man, you can't think of anything new? You think we still in Trinidad? This is London, man, this is London. The people want calypso on topical subject.'

'That is only the first verse,' Mango say, 'I am coming to the Suez' issue.'

And Mango, as if he get an inspiration, start to extemporise on Nasser and Eden and how he will give them the dope – the best thing is to pass the ships round the Cape of Good Hope.

'Like you have something there,' Hotboy concede, and he begin to hum a little tune.

Well in fifteen minutes time, in that tailor shop in the East End, the two boys had a calypso shaping up, and it wasn't a bad number, either.

Rahamut and the English assistant he have come and stand up listening, and when the calypso finish singing the English fellar say: 'That is one of the best calypsos I ever heard.'

But Rahamut say: 'Why you don't shut your mouth? What you English people know about calypso?'

'Well Rahamut what you think of it, eh?' Mango ask.

Rahamut want to say yes, it good, but he beating about the bush, he hemming and he hawing, he saying: 'Well, it so-so,' and 'It not so bad,' and 'I hear a lot of worse ones.'

But the English fellar who does assist Rahamut, he like the tune too bad, he only slapping Mango and Hotboy on the back and saying how he never hear a calypso like that. He swinging his hands in the air while he talking, and his hand hit Rahamut hand and Rahamut get a prick with a needle he was holding.

Well Rahamut put the finger in his mouth and suck it, and he turn round and start to abuse the English fellar, asking him if he don't know people does get blood poisoning with needle prick.

Hotboy really impressed with the words Mango think up, and he begin to have dreams again about a comeback: he could hear this calypso playing all about in London, and people going wild when they hear it.

And as if he could read Hotboy mind, the Mango realise that it was now or never if he going to tap Hotboy, so he turn to him and say softly: 'Hotboy, things really hard with me these days, you know. Why you don't lend me another ten, and make it a pound I have for you?'

Hotboy have a piece of paper before him and he writing down the calypso and concentrating hard on it: he tell Mango, 'Yes, yes,' not even realising what it is that Mango say.

'You hear that Rahamut?' Mango say quickly. 'You give me the ten, as Hotboy busy with the calypso, and afterwards he will fix you up.'

'I don't believe Hotboy hear what you say at all,' Rahamut cagey.

'You didn't hear for yourself?' Mango begin to push Rahamut and the English fellar out of the backroom. 'Leave him alone to concentrate on the number, don't interrupt him at all.'

In the front of the tailor shop big argument start up between Mango and Rahamut. Rahamut saying he sure that Hotboy didn't hear what Mango say, and Mango asking Rahamut if he deaf, if he didn't hear Hotboy say yes, yes.

In the end Mango manage to get the ten from Rahamut and he peel off fast, to hustle a cuppa and a hot pie.

About half an hour later Hotboy come to the front of the shop and ask: 'Which part Mango gone?'

'Mango gone,' Rahamut say, 'and I give him ten shillings for you. You better give it to me now before you forget.'

'Mango gone!' Hotboy repeat. 'You give him ten shillings for me! What you talking about?'

'John,' Rahamut turn to the English fellar, 'you didn't witness everything?'

But the English fellar start to get on cagey too, he see this sort of thing happening plenty times before and he don't want to become involved in any arguments the boys have.

'I was busy,' he say, and he went on sewing.

All the argue Rahamut argue Hotboy won't give him the ten. And that is as much as I know of the ballad. The other evening, liming in Marble Arch, I bounce up with Mango and he tell me that he went to see Hotboy and Hotboy tell him that he sell the calypso.

But up to now I can't hear it playing or singing anywhere, though I sure the number was really hearts, and would make some money for the boys if it catch on and sell.

Working the Transport

ONE TIME a fellar name Small Change get a work with London Transport. Small Change not really his name, but that is how all the boys know him as. I mean, you could know a fellar good, owe him money, or he owe you, go all about with him, and the both of you good, good friends, and yet if a day don't come when it really necessary to know what his true name is, he would dead and you still calling him Small Change.

Small Change hail from Barbados. You know where Barbados is? You don't? Well that is your hard luck. Anyway you must be read in the papers about how London Transport send men down there in the West Indies to get fellars to work on the tube and bus, and it look as if they like Barbadians, because they didn't go to any other islands: they just get some of the boys from Little England – that is what they call Barbados down there – and bring them up to work the transport.

At the time Small Change was working on a barge what used to go out to the big ships and bring in goods. He used to handle a oar so big that two-three fellars had to handle one oar.

When Small Change get the wire that they recruiting fellars to go to England and work, he left the barge same time and went home and put on some clean clothes and went to the office where they was recruiting these fellars.

'Can you drive?' they ask Change.

'Me? Drive?' Change smile and try to make his face look like he driving bus ever since he born. 'I was born behind a wheel.'

'Have you got your licence?'

'Yes, but not right here. I could go back home for it, though, if you want.'

'Driving in London isn't like driving in Barbados, you know.' The Englishman lean back in his chair, smoking a Lighthouse, which is the Barbadian equivalent to a Woods.

Change didn't deign to say anything to that, he just wait.

'How about your education?'

'Codrington College,' Change say. Change never went to school, but he call the name of one of the best college in that part of the world, and hope for the best.

'Have you got any recommendations?'

Change wasn't sure what the word mean, so he say quickly: 'No, but I could get some if you want.'

Well in the end Change find himself on a ship going to England. I mean, when you have ambition you have to play boldface and brazen, otherwise you get no place at all. It have fellars who get to the top only playing boldface, telling people they could do this and that when they don't know Adam from Eve. Change was always like that from small, only, he more boldface than ambitious, that's why he was only rowing them big barge instead of holding down a smart work in the island.

Anyway, Change come to London city, with Alipang, All-Fours, Catch-as-Catch-Can, Jackfish and a set of other fellars what get work with London Transport. (I sure you must be see All-Fours already – he have a work conducting in a bus, he only have eight fingers in all.)

Coming up on the ship, Change get the other fellars to gen him up on addition and subtraction, and he rig up a contraption like a car, with steering wheel and gear and clutch and brakes, and all the time the ship coming to England Change sitting there behind the wheel learning from one of the boys how to drive.

Of course, when the ship reach England it wasn't long before they find out that Change don't know anything about driving. In the garage a test tell him to move a bus, and Change get in as cool as anything, sit down, start the engine, press the clutch, race the engine, and throw in a reverse gear by mistake and back the bus up against the wall and give it a big dent right where it had an advertisement for binoculars, besides breaking up the glass in the back window where does have the names of the places where the bus going to.

Afterwards Jackfish tell him: 'Man, I warn you all the time I teaching you on the ship, that these buses in London funny. And you mean you don't know how to put in a reverse?'

'The buses really funny,' Change say. 'Upstairs and down-stairs, and I don't too like the view when you sit down in the driver seat.'

Jackfish say: 'You better try conducting old man.'

So Change say he prefer to conduct instead of drive, and they put him on a course to learn the ropes. Everything they teach Change, went in one ear and out the other. Change not paying any particular attention: he studying a little thing that he get in with down by the Elephant, where he living. When Change get in with this thing she ask him: 'Can you rock 'n' roll?'

'Can I rock 'n' roll!' Change repeat. 'Child, that dance out of fashion where I come from, we used to do that two years ago. The latest thing now is hip 'n' hit. You mean to say is only now you all doing rock 'n' roll in London?'

'Hip 'n' hit?' the blonde say, puzzled. 'What's that?'

'I'll show you Saturday night, when we go dancing,' Change say.

So while the transport people trying to learn Change how to conduct, Change studying some kind of newfangle step, and when elevenses come he went to the other boys and tell them how he have to invent a new dance else the West Indies would be let down.

Catch-as-Catch-Can who used to lime out regularly at all the dances it have in Barbados, tell Change to take it easy.

'You want to learn some new steps?' Catch say. 'Give me a beat.'

So Change sit down on the platform on a bus and start to beat the side, and Alipang finish drinking tea and hitting the empty cup with the spoon, while Jackfish keeping time on the bar it have what you does hold on to when you going in the bus. And Catch dancing some fancy steps, a kind of Gene Kelly mixup with some mambo and samba and some real carnival 'break-away', which is what they call the dancing the people dance in the islands when is carnival time.

'This bus have a good tone,' Change say, looking up to see what number bus it is, as if the number make a difference.

'You watching?' Catch say. 'See if you could manage that.'

So Change get up and start to do as Catch was doing, and Catch saying no, not that way, and showing him how.

Them other English fellars gather around enjoying the slackness, because you know how they themselves cargoo, they don't know how to shake a leg or how to get hep, until the fellar who was in charge finish his tea and come and say: 'All right fellows, break it up.'

Change get a 196 bus to conduct, from Tufnell Park in the north to Norwood Junction in the south. The first morning he went to work, the bus get about a quarter-mile from the garage before Change realise that he left all his tickets behind. He had was to ring the bell and stop the bus and go out and tell the driver what happen. This time so all them people hustling to get to work and want to know what happening: in the end they had to get out and wait for another bus while the driver drive back to the garage for Change to collect the tickets.

Meantime he learning all the teddy boys and teddy girls in the Elephant to dance hip 'n' hit, until it become a real craze south of the river.

It was ruction in the town when the teddies start up on this new dance that Change introduce, and pretty soon everybody forget about 'rock 'n' roll' and start to concentrate on 'hip 'n' hit', and the old Change figuring out if he can't make something on the side by giving lessons after work.

Meantime, too, he get tired of running up and down the stairs in the bus to punch ticket, and having to work the old brains hard to figure out how much change to give, two and a half, tenpence, one and four, and all them funny ways the English have with money, instead of a flat dollar and cents.

One evening in a rush hour he surprise to pick up Alipang by Waterloo station.

'What happening boy, which part you working?' Change ask.

'Underground, boy,' Alipang say.

'Underground! In the tubes and them?'

'Yes. I guarding at one of the stations.'

'Alipang, is a hard work boy? It hard as conducting bus?'

'Easy as kissing hand, man. All you have to do is say mind the doors, right, all change, and so on.'

'I tired with this bus work, man. I think I going to ask for a transfer to the tubes and them. Where you going?'

'Norwood Junction. That is one and two?'

'It used to be. Is one and four now, papa,' Change say, punching two tickets, one for the one and the other for the four.

'L.T. bleeding money in this country,' Alipang observe.

Two months later Change was working in the underground, patrolling the platform in a station and calling out 'Mind the doors!' and 'Right!' Things look like they was going all right, until they move Change from the station where he was and put him Marble Arch to work, on the Central Line. Well somehow or other Change get the idea that is 'all change' at the Arch for every train that pass, and the first morning he on duty he call out 'All change!' for a train that was going through to Liverpool Street, and cause big confusion in the tube station when everybody come off the train and stand up waiting for the other one. In fact, what Change do was he cause a dislocation of the schedules of all the trains on the Central Line, from West Ruislip to Ongar, and how he didn't get fire that time was a wonder. When L.T. ask him for an explanation, Change beg for another chance. 'This country so cold,' Change say, 'I can't think properly. But I will get accustom soon.'

'This is your last chance,' L.T. warn him, and put him to work collecting tickets. Change like that too bad. He sitting down on top an escalator all day long and collecting tickets, and sometimes when things dullish he clipping the tickets for passengers going down.

Well, it ain't have a lot more episode to tell you about Change, except how he lose the work at last. I mean L.T. really try with that test.

At this stage Change was settling down nicely to punching ticket at the top of the escalator, but something had to spoil it, and you know what – woman. As soon as a man start to prosper a little and catch himself in this world, woman come in and cause misery. All over the world is the same thing, even in London. And as soon as they come they start to make bassa-bassa, which is to say, anything they touch they put blight on it and cause trouble.

Was the little blonde what Change learn to do the hip 'n' hit. The girl behind Change all the time, and won't leave him in peace. And climax come one afternoon. Things was dullish, and a smart chick was coming up the escalator, and Change stop the thing and begin to talk, trying to make a date. Well little Blondie come up same time and start to make big noise, asking Change if that is what he does be doing behind her back, trying to date other women, and she start to tussle with the chick, and poor Change trying to part them and soothe things. In the scramble Change cap fall on the escalator and begin to go down, and Change start after it. Well same time, as the gods would have it, a L.T. inspector coming up on the other side, and he see all what happening.

This time they didn't ask Change for an explanation. They just fire him.

'Never mind, they are taking on workers in King's Cross,' Blondie tell Change afterwards.

But Change give she a clout behind she head and went to mourn to the other boys about what happen.

Waiting for Aunty to Cough

IT HAD a late lime what few of the boys acquainted with. That don't mean to say was anything exclusive, but as far as I know Brackley was the only fellar who get in with a thing that living far from London, and had was to see the piece home every night, going out of the city and coming back late, missing bus and train and having to hustle or else stay stranded in one of them places behind God back.

I mean, some people might say a place like where Brackley used to go ain't far, and argue even that it still included in London, but to the city boys, as soon as you start to hit Clapham Common or Chiswick or Mile End or Highgate, that mean you living in the country, and they out to give you tone, like: 'Mind you miss the last bus home, old man,' and, 'When next you coming to town?' or, 'You could get some fresh eggs for me where you living?'

Well Brackley in fact settle down nicely in Central, a two and ten room in Ladbroke Grove, with easy communications for liming out in the evenings after work, and the old Portobello road near by to buy rations like saltfish and red beans and pig foot and pig tail. And almost every evening he would meet the boys and they would lime by the Arch, or the Gate, and have a cup of coffee (it have place like stupidness now all over London selling coffee, you notice?) and coast a talk and keep a weather eye open for whatever might appear on the horizon.

But a time come, when the boys begin to miss Brackley.

'Anybody see Brackley?'

'I ain't see Brackley a long time, man. He must be move.'

'He uses to be in this coffee shop regular, but these days I can't see him at all.'

All this time, Brackley on one of them green trains you does catch in Charing Cross or Waterloo, taking a ride and seeing the girl home.

Though Brackley living in London for eight years, is as if he start to discover a new world. Brackley never hear name like what he reading as they pass them stations – Gypsy Hill, Penge West, Forest Hill.

'You sure we on the right train?' Brackley frighten like hell the first time, feeling as if they going to Scotland or something. 'How far from London you say this place is?'

'It is in London, I keep telling you,' the girl say patiently.

'All of this is London?' Brackley look out and see a station name Honor Oak Park. Houses fading away and down there real grim as if is a place far out in the country.

'Yes,' Beatrice say.

'And every day, you have to come all this way to work in London?'

'Yes.'

'Oh, you must be one of those commuter people I read about in the papers.'

Brackley look at his wristwatch. 'I don't like this lime,' he say.

'Oh, you'll get accustomed to it,' Beatrice say. 'It is like nothing to me now.'

'I wonder what the boys doing in the coffee shop in town,' Brackley mutter.

'That is all you ever worry about – wasting your time,' Beatrice start to sulk.

'It ain't have no high spots this side of the world?' Brackley ask. 'If it have, we could go out down here instead of staying in London and coming home late every night.'

'You know I like to go out in the city,' Beatrice pout. 'The only place we could go to down here is near to Croydon.'

'Croydon!' Brackley repeat. 'Where the aeroplanes come from all over the world? You mean to say we so far from London?'

'There are frequent trains,' Beatrice say anxiously.

'Frequent trains!' Brackley repeat. 'Frequent planes, you mean! I don't like the lime at all.'

But all the same, Brackley like the thing and he was seeing she home every night.

Well he start to extend his geographical knowledge from the time he going out with Beatrice, and when he was explaining his absence from the city to the boys, he making it sound as if is a grand lime.

'Man,' he boasting, 'you-all don't know London! You think London is the Gate and the Arch and Trafalgar Square, but them places is nothing. You ever hear about Honor Oak Rise?'

'Which part that is, behind God back?'

'That is a place in London, man! I mean, look at it this way. You live in London so long, and up to now you don't know where that is. You see what I mean?'

'Man Brackley, you only full of guile. This time so that woman have you stupid and travelling all over the country, when you could be liming here. You staying tonight? It have two sharp things does come for coffee here – I think they from Sweden, and you know over there ain't have no inhibition.'

'I can't stay tonight.'

'Today is Saturday, no night bus.'

But Brackley in hot with Beatrice at this stage and that ain't worrying him. What happen that night was he find himself walking to Kent afterwards, thinking that he was on the way to London, and he would have found himself picking hops or something if a fellar didn't put him right.

One night Brackley was taking a cuppa and a roll in a little place it have near Charing Cross, what does stay open all night for stragglers like him. The set-up is this: three-four frowsy women, and some tests who look as if they only come out at night. I mean, if you really want to meet some characters, is to lime out there by the Embankment after midnight, and you sure to meet some individuals.

That night, two fellars playing dominoes. A group stand up round a fire that they light with wood to keep warm. Suddenly a big commotion start, because the police take Olive and a test say it serve her right.

A woman start to 'buse the fellar who say it serve Olive right.

'What do you know about it?' the woman snarl. 'Keep your ——ing mouth shut.'

She start to scratch her thigh. Same time another woman come hustling up with the stale news that the police take Olive.

'Yes,' the first woman say, 'and this bastard here say that it served her right.' She turn to the fellar again, 'Keep your ——ing mouth shut,' she say, though the fellar ain't saying anything.

Suddenly she turn on Brackley and start to 'buse him, saying that he was responsible. Poor Brackley ain't have a clue what the woman talking about, but three-four frowsy-looking sports gather around him and want to beat him up.

Brackley ease away and start to go up by Whitehall, and the starlings kicking up hell on the sides of the tall buildings, and is almost three o'clock in the morning and he thinking what a hell of a thing life is, how he never ever hear about any Olive and look how them women wanted to beat him up.

Well to get back to the heart of the ballad, one rainy night Brackley and Beatrice went theatre, and theatre over late, and they catch the last train out of town. While they on the train – and Brackley like a regular commuter these days, reading the *Standard* while Beatrice catching up on some knitting – Beatrice suddenly open her handbag and say: 'Gosh, I think I've lost my key!'

'You could always get another one,' Brackley say, reading How The Other Half Laughs.

'You don't understand,' Beatrice moan. 'Aunty is always complaining about my coming in late, and by the time we get home it will be long after midnight, and the door will be shut.'

'Ring the bell,' Brackley say, laughing at a joke in the paper.

'I daren't wake Aunty at that hour,' Beatrice say, putting aside the knitting to worry better.

'Don't worry, I will open a window for you,' Brackley say.

But when they get to where Beatrice living she was still worrying what to do. She tell Brackley to wait by the gate. She went inside and pick up a tiny pebble and throw at the window, which was on the first floor. It make a sound ping! but nothing happen. After a little while she throw another one ping! but still nothing happen.

Brackley stand up there watching her.

She turn to Brackley helplessly. 'I can't wake Aunty,' she say.

Brackley open the gate and come inside and pick up a big brick from the garden to pelt at the people glass window. Beatrice barely had time to hold his hand.

'Are you mad?' she say in a fierce whisper.

'Well,' Brackley say, 'you don't want to get inside?'

'You are making too much noise already,' Beatrice whisper. 'I will have to stay on the steps until Aunty gets up.'

'What time is that?' Brackley ask.

'About six o'clock,' Beatrice say. 'She is an early riser.'

'You mean to say,' Brackley say, 'you spending the night here in the damp? Why you don't make a big noise and wake she up?'

'No no,' Beatrice say quickly, 'we mustn't make any noise. The neighbours are very troublesome. Let us wait here until Aunty gets up. She is restless at night. When I hear her coughing I will throw another stone.'

So Brackley and Beatrice sit down on the wet steps, waiting for Aunty to cough.

One o'clock come and gone, two o'clock come and gone.

Three o'clock rain start to pelt slantways and fall on the steps wetting Brackley. This time so, as Brackley look around, the world grim. Rain and fog around him, and Beatrice sleeping on his shoulder.

He shake her.

Beatrice open her eyes and say, 'What is it, did you hear Aunty cough?'

'No. It look as if her cold get better, I don't think she going to cough tonight at all.'

'She always coughs in the night. As soon as she does I will throw some stones again.'

'Why you don't make a big noise and finish with it? Back home in Trinidad, you think this could happen? Why – '

'Hush, you are speaking too loudly. I told you it would cause trouble with the neighbours.'

'Why you don't wake up the people on the ground floor?'

'Nobody is there – they work nights.'

'I ain't even have a cigarette,' Brackley grumble, wondering what the boys doing, if they get in with the two girls from Sweden and gone to sleep in a nice warm room.

Beatrice went back to sleep, using poor Brackley as pillow.

Four o'clock come, five o'clock come, and still Brackley waiting for Aunty to cough and she wouldn't cough. This time so he have a sizeable stone in his hand and he make up his mind that the moment Aunty cough he going to fling the stone at the window even if he wake up everybody in the street. Sleep killing Brackley but the doorway small and he bend up there like a piece of wire, catching cramp and unable to shift position. In fact, between five and halfpast Brackley think he hear Aunty cough and he make to get up and couldn't move, all the joints frozen in the damp and cold.

He shake Beatrice roughly. 'Aunty cough,' he say.

'I didn't hear,' Beatrice say.

'I hear,' Brackley say, and he stretch out slowly and get up. Brackley augment the stone he had with three others and he fling his hand back and he pelt the stones on the people glass window before Beatrice know what he doing.

Well glass cracks and break and splinters fly all about and the noise sound as if the glasshouse in Kew Gardens falling down. Same time Aunty start one set of coughing.

'You see?' Brackley say, 'I tell you Aunty was coughing!'

'You fool!' Beatrice say. 'Look what you have done! You had better go quickly before you cause further trouble.'

And before Brackley know what happening Beatrice hustle him out to the pavement and shut the gate.

Well a kind of fore-day light was falling at that hour of the morning and when Aunty fling open the window to see what happening, she see Brackley stand up out there. Only, she not so sure, because Brackley blend in nicely with the kind of half-light half-dark. But all the same, Aunty begin to scream murder and thief.

Brackley take off as if he on the Ascot racecourse.

Some nights later he tell the boys the episode, making it sound like a good joke though at the time he was frighten like hell. But that was a mistake he make, because since that time whenever the boys see him they hailing out:

'Brackley! You still waiting for Aunty to cough?'

Eraser's Dilemma

IF YOU ARE one of the hustlers on Route 12 I don't know how you could fail to notice Eraser, he such a cheerful conductor. And if you look good, under the regulation uniform, you might notice him wearing a happy nylon shirt, green, with red stripes.

That shirt is Eraser's pet wear, and if you have a bus fare and want to take a ride – in fact, the beauty is you might be on his bus now even as you reading this – I will give you the ballad about that happy shirt.

To Londoners a bus is a bus. If you queueing for one and another come along, you just hop in, as long as it take you where you want to go. The red double-deckers come as nothing, a sight you seeing day in and day out.

Eraser had a different feeling about them. Like how a sailor love his ship, so Eraser love his bus, and it hurt him to go off duty and hand over to another conductor who mightn't feel the way he do. Seeing that he couldn't be sure of always working the same bus, Eraser adopt the route and determine to make it the nicest one in London.

And in point of fact, though I wouldn't say that one man able to work a route smoothly or even one bus on the route for that matter, it is true that from the time Eraser begin to work on Route 12, a change for the better take place.

One or two letter even appear in the newspaper complimenting L.T. on the improvement, and once a lady that was helped on and off a bus write to say how wonderful these West Indians were, that she notice they was extremely kind

and polite and did their job well. (I only telling you what the lady say.)

Them kind of letter, you don't see them often, but whenever one appear concerning his route Eraser keep the clipping to send home to St Vincent to his grandmother.

Once he send a photo of the bus he working on. He take it out in the garage, with him hugging the bonnet like how you see them jockeys holding on to the horse neck when they come in first, and he send the photo home.

You should hear them in St Vincent, talking about it, wanting to know why the bus so high, and why it have upstairs and downstairs.

Well, when Eraser on duty, it ain't have nothing like woman standing in his bus at all. From the time that begin to happen Eraser saying out loud: 'Which gallant Englishman will give this lady his seat?'

I don't have to tell you what happen when Eraser say that. Everybody get quiet as if they in church. A test working in the City, with bowler and brolly, bury his face in the *Financial Times*. Some fellars looking out the window and admiring the London scenery. Other fellars as if they deaf.

'Come now,' you should hear Eraser, 'surely there are gentlemen on my bus?'

And eventually one or two fellars would get up, glaring at Eraser, and all the women in the bus would look at him and smile among themselves.

Well, it had one of these old ladies what used to catch Eraser bus as regular as clockwork, and he always there to help her on and off. And they would exchange the usual about the weather, and how are you today, and that sort of thing, and if trade not very busy she would tell Eraser to sing a calypso, and he would oblige, because he is that sort of fellar. I mean, all the time he working he whistling or singing, spreading sunshine in the bus. Nothing could dampen the old Eraser.

What happen one day is this. The old lady get on the bus

with a parcel, but when she get off she forget to take it. Other passengers see the parcel, but you know how it is in London, everybody lock-up and suspicious, nobody ain't say a word.

Eraser decide to keep the parcel instead of handing it in at the garage, feeling it would be nice to give it to her himself the next day when she catch the bus, and save her the trouble of going quite to Baker Street to the Lost Property Office.

He tell Jack, the driver, who was a steady, unimaginative fellar about it. Jack just shrug and say if he wanted to take the chance it was his business.

Well the next day when the bus get to the stop where the old lady uses to get on, no old lady there. Eraser get uneasy. These English people, they have habits, and Eraser know she would wait for his bus as she always did all the months he on the route.

He went home worried, but thinking he would see she the next day.

Next day come. No old lady.

Eraser went to Jack when they was having a break for tea at the garage.

'You remember that parcel,' Eraser say. 'Well, the old lady ain't turn up since.'

'Do you know her name?' Jack ask.

'No,' Eraser say.

'Isn't there any address on the parcel?' Jack ask.

'No,' Eraser say.

'You should have handed it in the first day,' Jack say.

'I will wait one more day, maybe she is sick,' Eraser say.

Jack shrug and went on with his elevenses.

Well the third day come. By the bus stop, no old lady.

Eraser begin to sweat. He even allow a lady to stand up for five minutes before he realise she should be sitting instead of one of the hulky fellars in the bus. Just because he wanted to do a good turn, it look like trouble catch up with him.

Eraser get off duty at twelve o'clock and didn't even bother about lunch. He went to the bus stop which part the old lady uses to wait. At this stage the parcel like live coal in his hand, and he praying that he would meet somebody who know her.

But three-four people that he stop and ask, none of them know who he mean.

'It can't be far from here,' Eraser say to himself, combing the district around the bus-stop.

And this time, he imagining all sorts of things, how L.T. would want to know why he didn't turn in the parcel, if he didn't know the rules and regulations. They might even think he wanted to thief the parcel. What he would say to all that?

And so he in this panic as he searching, because he like his job and things was going all right until this had to happen.

At last, in a small sweet-shop, he strike some luck. Yes, the attendant think she know who he talking about, an old lady called Miss Bellflent, living at No. 5.

Eraser take off in this street looking for No. 5, and he ring all the buzzers it had on the door when he get there. He could hardly ask the landlady for Miss Bellflent when she come to the door.

'Miss Bellflent?' the landlady say. 'Why, she left a few days ago. She isn't staying here any more.'

Eraser see himself in big trouble, out of a job, no bus to conduct.

'Do you know where she lives now?' he ask weakly.

'No.'

In his mind Eraser begin taking off his uniform for the last time. Things always hard on the boys, and now he was having his share. He could imagine what everybody would be saying, oh yes they are cheerful and work well, but after all . . .

And the landlady, as if she could see how important it was, and noticing the disappointment on Eraser's face, say: 'Wait a minute,' and she went inside.

When she come back she give Eraser a address on a piece of paper. 'Try there,' she said. Eraser was making up the road before he remember to turn round and shout: 'Thank you!'

At last it look like there was still hope, and he race to the address, and when he knock and Miss Bellflent open the door, he feel to kiss her.

'Why, it's you!' Miss Bellflent say. 'Do come in!'

And when Eraser get inside, she tell him to sit down and she put the tea-kettle on the fire right away.

'You must have a cup of tea,' she said kindly.

'I only came about this parcel which you forgot on the bus.' Eraser say, throwing the world off his shoulders, and putting down the parcel on the table and wiping his hands, as if he too glad it was finish with.

'But I meant it for you!' Miss Bellflent say in a matter-of-fact way. 'I thought I wrote a note on the box. How absent-minded of me.'

'For me?' Eraser stand up by the table as if he stun.

'Yes, of course!' Miss Bellflent say, pouring out the tea. 'Go on then, aren't you going to open it?'

Eraser touch the parcel as if he frighten. He loosen the string and open a box.

Inside, it had a happy nylon shirt, green, with red stripes.

Brackley and the Bed

ONE EVENING Brackley was cruising round by the Embankment looking for a soft bench to rest his weary bones, and to cogitate on the ways of life. The reason for that, and the reason why the boys begin to call him Rockabye, you will find out as the ballad goes on.

Brackley hail from Tobago, which part they have it to say Robinson Crusoe used to hang out with Man Friday. Things was brown in that island and he make for England and manage to get a work and was just settling down when bam! he get a letter from his aunt saying that Teena want to come England too.

Teena was Brackley distant cousin and they was good friends in Tobago. In fact, the other reason why Brackley hustle from the island is because it did look like he and Teena was heading for a little married thing, and Brackley run.

Well, right away he write aunty and say no, no, because he have a feeling this girl would make botheration if she come England. The aunt write back to say she didn't mean to say that Teena want to come England, but that Teena left Tobago for England already.

Brackley hold his head and bawl. And the evening the boat train come in at Waterloo, he went there and start 'busing she right away not waiting to ask how the folks at home was or anything.

'What you doing in London?' Brackley ask as soon as Teena step off the train. 'What you come here for, eh? Even though I write home to say things real hard?'

'What happen, you buy the country already?' Teena sheself

giving tit for tat right away. 'You ruling England now? The Queen abdicate?'

'You know where you going?' Brackley say. 'You know where you is? You know what you going to do?'

'I am going straight to the Colonial Office,' Teena say.

'What you think the Colonial Office is, eh? You think they will do anything for you? You have a god-father working there?'

Well, they argue until in the end Brackley find himself holding on to Teena suitcase and they on the way to the little batchy he have in Golders Green at the time.

When they get there Teena take one look at the room and sniff. 'But look at the state you have this room in! You ain't ashamed of yourself?'

'Listen,' Brackley say, 'you better don't let me and you have contention. I know this would of happen when you come.'

Teena start squaring up the room brisk-brisk.

'It making cold,' she say, putting chair this way and table that way and turning everything upside down for poor Brackley. 'How you does keep warm? Where the gas fire I hear so much about?'

Brackley grudgingly put a shilling in the meter and light the gas.

'What you have to eat?' But even as she asking she gone in the cupboard and begin pulling out rations that Brackley had stow away to see him through the winter. Brackley as if he mesmerise, stand up there watching her as she start up a peas and rice on the gas ring.

'You better go easy with them rations,' he say. 'I not working now and money don't grow on tree here as in Tobago.'

When they was eating Teena say: 'Well you have to get a job right away. You was always a lazy fellar.'

'Keep quiet,' Brackley say, enjoying the meal that Teena cook in real West Indian fashion – the first good meal he ever had in London. 'You don't know nothing.'

'First thing tomorrow morning,' Teena say. 'What time you get up?'

'About nine – ten,' Brackley say vaguely.

'Well is six o'clock tomorrow morning, bright and early as the cock crow.'

'You don't hear cock crowing in London,' Brackley say. Then he drop the spoon he was eating with. 'Six o'clock! You must be mad! Six o'clock like midnight in the winter, and people still sound asleep.'

'Six o'clock,' Teena say.

Brackley finish eating and begin to smoke, whistling a calypso softly, as if he in another world and not aware of Teena at all.

'Ah well,' he say, stretching by the fire, 'that wasn't a bad meal. Look, I will give you some old blankets and you could wrap up that coat and use as a pillow – you could sleep on the ground in that corner ...'

'*Me*? On the floor? You not ashamed?'

'Well, is only one bed here as you see ...'

'I using the bed.'

'Girl, is winter, and if you think I going to sleep in the corner with two old blanket and wake up stiff ...'

But, in the end, was Brackley who crouch up in the corner, and Teena sound asleep in the bed.

It look to Brackley like he hardly shut his eyes before Teena was shaking him.

'Get up,' Teena say, 'six o'clock.'

Brackley start to curse.

'None of that,' Teena say. 'No bad language when I around.'

Teena move around fast and give Brackley breakfast and make him dress and get out on the cold streets mumbling, 'Get a job, get a job,' before he knew what happening.

It was only about 10 o'clock, when he was washing dishes in a café where he get a work, that Brackley realise what was happening to him.

When he get home in the evening, Teena have screen put up around the bed and everything spick and span, and Brackley don't know where to look even for chair to sit down.

'I see you make yourself at home,' he sav maliciously.

'And what you think?' Teena flares.

'The boys does come here sometimes for a little rummy.'

'None of that now.'

'And sometimes a girl-friend visit me.'

'None of that now.'

'So you taking over completely.'

'Aunty say to look after you.'

'Why the hell you come England, eh?'

Well, a pattern begin to form as the weeks go by, but the main thing that have Brackley worried is the bed. Every night he curl up in the corner shivering, and by the time he doze off: 'Six o'clock, get up, you have to go to work.'

Brackley ain't sleep on bed for weeks. The thing like an obsession with him. He window-shopping on the way home and looking at them bed and soft mattress on show and closing his eyes and sighing. Single divan, double divan, put-you-up, put-you-down – all makes and sizes he looking at.

One night when frost was forming on the window pane Brackley wake up and find he couldn't move.

'Teena.'

'What?'

'You sleeping?'

'Yes.'

'Teena, you want to get married?'

'Married? To who?'

'To me.'

'What for?'

'So-I-could-sleep-in-the-bed – I mean, well, we uses to know one another good in Tobago, and now that you here in London, what you think?'

'Well, all right, but you have to change your ways.'

'Yes, Teena.'

'And no 'foolishness when we married. You come home straight from work. And I don't want you looking at no white girls.'

'Yes, Teena.'

No sooner said than done. Brackley hustle Teena off to the registry office as soon as things was fixed, thinking only how nice the bed would be after the hard floor and the cold, with Teena to help keep him warm.

'What about honeymoon?' Teena say after the ceremony.

'In the summer,' Brackley say. 'Let we go home. I am tired and I feel I could sleep for weeks.'

'Bracks,' Teena say as they was coming away, 'I have a nice surprise for you. Guess who coming to London this evening?'

'Father Christmas,' Brackley says yawning.

'No. Aunty. I write telling her to come up, as the room not so small and we could manage until we get another place. And then she and me could get a work too, and that will help.'

'You putting hell 'pon jackass back,' Brackley moan. But it was only when they reach home that a great fear come to Brackley. He had was to sit down in a chair before he could talk.

'But Teena,' he say quietly, 'we ain't have no place for Aunty to sleep?'

'Don't worry,' Teena say, 'She can sleep with me until we find another place.'

If Winter Comes

IT DOES HAVE certain times in London, when a kind of blight descend on the boys. Everybody hard-up, and you can't get a ease-up from your best friend. And the point is, it don't happen in summer, when at least you have a little sunshine and a daffodil or tulip to console you, but in them grim days of winter when night fall on the city from three o'clock in the afternoon, and you looking all about in the fog for a friend to borrow a shilling for the gas meter.

But everybody cagey-cagey, men looking at you with suspicion from the time you appear in the distance, and some fellars, as if they have radar, could sense when a hard-up test on the horizon, and right away they begin to limp and cry big water, so that by the time you get near you realise it have a situation here that far worse than yours.

I mean, when a fellar like Brakes can't manage a borrow, you could imagine what the situation like. Because Brakes have a way, he would mamaguile you with all kind of sweet-talk, and hark back to the old days in the islands, and when he have the memories well-stirred, of a sudden he would come out with something like: 'Lend me four shillings and five-pence ha'penny, boy – I in a jam.'

Notice the sum he ask for. When Brakes making a tap he always asking for a particular sum as if he have something direct in mind.

But no approach was successful that season.

'These look like evil days' Brakes say to himself. 'What happen to everybody? I will have to think of something.'

He had to put the old brains to work, because Mavis was

after a coat that she see in a store in Oxford Street (the same place where Nina bounce some hats and cause havoc in international relationships) and this coat cost exactly £10. But as far as Brakes concern it might as well cost £500.

'Same reason I don't like to come window-shopping with you,' Brakes grumble. 'Everything you see you want.'

'I must have that coat, Brakes,' Mavis say, as if she didn't hear him at all.

'You know I ain't have a work now,' Brakes say.

'If you love me, you would get that coat for me, Brakes.'

Well I ain't fooling you, but woman really bad, *oui*. Mavis stick behind Brakes like a leech, until he had was to promise to get it for her before the next week out.

Brakes stand up by Tottenham Court Tube station pondering the situation when she left him. And the only think he could think of, is to get some fellars to take a hand in a sou-sou. That is a thing like this: about ten of you decide to give a pound each every week, and the £10 would make the rounds of each person, and at the end of the ten weeks each one will have had £10.

But Brakes figuring on running a sou-sou where he don't have to put anything in. He planning to get ten fellars beside himself, and don't tell them is really eleven and not ten. And naturally he takes the first £10 collected for himself. After that things would go all right until it come to the last week, when two fellars would be expecting to collect, 'and by that time something bound to turn up,' Brakes tell himself.

Well, he get eight of the boys and two English fellars, and he went around like a landlord the first payday and collect the ten, and right after went and buy the coat for Mavis.

Mavis put on the coat and want to go West End right away. They cruise round by the Dilly, but everytime Mavis stop by a show window Brakes pull she away before she could say she want this and she want that.

'We haven't been to the theatre a long time,' Mavis observe, wanting to show off the new coat.

'The most you getting is a walk in Trafalgar Square,' Brakes say, feeling in his pockets and only clutching air, 'to watch the fountains spouting water.'

Well the weeks breeze by, and two days was to go for the last two fellars in the sou-sou to get the money, and Brakes wasn't nearer a work, much less the money.

He dress and went out in the last act of despair the boys resort to – looking for money in the streets. You don't know sometimes what your luck might be – you might spot a crumple-up pound note or a ten shilling somewhere on the pavement where people walking so fast that they ain't have time to look down.

Brakes have time – in fact his face rivet-down to the ground, but he reach to them side streets in Soho and the most he find is two safety pin. That wasn't a happy hunting ground, because it have a lot of tests does be liming there and if anybody drop a note or even a tanner by accident, you could be sure it hardly have time settle on the ground before a test ups it.

But Brakes wasn't thinking where he going. He collide-up with a fellar who was in a hurry.

'What is all the rush, Chippy?' Brakes say, recognising a shady Englisher who live by gambling.

'I am on something hot,' Chippy say. 'I am off to put money on a sure horse.'

Brakes brain start to work tick-tock. 'What is the odds?' he ask Chippy.

'The odds are ten to one,' Chippy say. He make to move off, then he stop. 'Would you like me to put something on for you?' He pull Brakes to one side and talking in a whisper. 'Meet me here by three o'clock if you are interested.' And with that he takes off.

Well, by three o'clock Brakes hand Chippy a pound and remain sweating until the race finish. Praise the lord, the horse come in and Brakes see his worries over for the time being. All he had to do was collect the last hand and then pay off the two fellars.

The last man in the sou-sou was a Englisher, and as soon as he see Brakes he say: 'Something fishy seems to be going on. I understand that this sou-sou thing is finished, and I haven't had any money. I have been looking all over town for you.'

'Take it easy,' Brakes say. 'I have the money right here for you.'

The Englisher lick his thumb and count the money. 'It was a good experience,' he say, 'but count me out the next time.'

After that, the only worry was Mavis. Brakes take a trip to the nearest public library and spent some time reading poetry before he went to pick her up after work.

'Did you manage to borrow money for the sou-sou?' was the first thing she ask him, because Brakes did tell her everything but she couldn't help.

'I bet on a horse and it come in,' Brakes say.

'Where did you get the money to bet?'

'Well,' Brakes start to fidget. 'I had to get this money somehow. Anyway, don't worry.' Brakes trying hard to remember the poetry he read in the library. 'You know that nice poetry about if winter come, spring running a close second. It only have a few more weeks and then no more winter, and people won't need to put on any heavy clothes.'

'What is all that in aid of?' Mavis suspicious and pull Brakes to one side of the pavement and stand up.

'Well, you won't need that coat any more,' Brakes say. 'I tell you, spring is just around the corner.'

'What are you trying to say?' Mavis say impatiently.

'I sell the coat for a pound to get money to bet. It's quite mild now, you don't think?'

Though the day was really mild Mavis start to shiver as if she have ague.

'Sold my coat!' she say, holding on to her shoulders and trembling with imaginary cold. 'Why did you do that, Brakes?'

'I keep telling you about the poetry that say if winter come, spring racing a close second. Only a few more days and . . .'

Mavis ready to cry. 'I haven't had a new coat for years. What will I do when winter comes again?'

Brakes ponder the question for a moment.

'Don't worry,' he say brightly. 'I will run another sou-sou and buy one for you!'

The Cricket Match

THE TIME WHEN the West Indies cricket eleven come to England to show the Englishmen the finer points of the game, Algernon was working in a tyre factory down by Chiswick way, and he lambast them English fellars for so.

'That is the way to play the game,' he tell them, as the series went on and West Indies making some big score and bowling out them English fellars for duck and thing, 'you thought we didn't know how to play the game, eh? That is cricket, lovely cricket.'

And all day he singing a calypso that he make up about the cricket matches that play, ending up by saying that in the world of sport, is to wait until the West Indies report.

Well in truth and in fact, the people in this country believe that everybody who come from the West Indies at least like the game even if they can't play it. But you could take it from me that it have some tests that don't like the game at all, and among them was Algernon. But he see a chance to give the Nordics tone and he get all the gen on the matches and players, and come like an authority in the factory on cricket. In fact, the more they ask him the more convinced Algernon get that perhaps he have the talent of a Walcott in him only waiting for a chance to come out.

They have a portable radio hide away from the foreman and they listening to the score every day. And as the match going on you should hear Algernon: 'Yes, lovely stroke,' and 'That should have been a six,' and so on. Meanwhile, he picking up any round object that near to hand and making demonstration, showing them how Ramadhin does spin the ball.

'I bet you used to play a lot back home,' the English fellars tell him.

'Who, me?' Algernon say. 'Man, cricket is breakfast and dinner where I come from. If you want to learn about the game you must go down there. I don't want to brag,' he say, hanging his head a little, 'but I used to live next door to Ramadhin, and we used to teach one another the fine points.'

But what you think Algernon know about cricket in truth? The most he ever play was in the street, with a bat make from a coconut branch, a dry mango seed for ball, and a pitchoil tin for wicket. And that was when he was a boy, and one day he get lash with the mango seed and since that time he never play again.

But all day long in the factory, he and another West Indian fellar name Roy getting on as if they invent the game, and the more the West Indies eleven score, the more they getting on. At last a Englisher name Charles, who was living in the sub- urbs, say to Algernon one morning:

'You chaps from the West Indies are really fine cricketers. I was just wondering ... I play for a side where I live, and the other day I mentioned you and Roy to our captain, and he said why don't you organise an eleven and come down our way one Saturday for a match? Of course,' Charles went on earnestly, 'we don't expect to be good enough for you, but still, it will be fun.'

'Oh,' Algernon say airily, 'I don't know. I uses to play in firstclass matches, and most of the boys I know accustom to a real good game with strong opposition. What kind of pitch you have?'

'The pitch is good,' Charles say. 'Real English turf.'

Algernon start to hedge. He scratch his head. He say, 'I don't know. What you think about the idea, Roy?'

Roy decide to hem and leave Algernon to get them out of the mooch. He say, 'I don't know, either. It sound like a good idea, though.'

'See what you can do,' Charles say, 'and let me know this week.'

Afterwards in the canteen having elevenses Roy tell Algernon: 'You see what your big mouth get us into.'

'*My* big mouth!' Algernon say. 'Who it is say he bowl four top bats for duck one after the other in a match in Queen's Park oval in Port of Spain? Who it is say he score two hundred and fifty not out in a match against Jamaica?'

'Well to tell you the truth Algernon,' Roy say, now that they was down to brass tacks, 'I ain't play cricket for a long time. In fact, I don't believe I could still play.'

'Me too, boy,' Algernon say. 'I mean, up here in England you don't get a chance to practise or anything. I must be out of form.'

They sit down there in the canteen cogitating on the problem.

'Anyway,' Roy say, 'it look as if we will have to hustle an eleven somehow. We can't back out of it now.'

'I studying,' Algernon say, scratching his head. 'What about Eric, you think he will play?'

'You could ask him, he might. And what about Williams? And Wilky? And Heads? Those boys should know how to play.'

'Yes, but look at trouble to get them! Wilky working night and he will want to sleep. Heads is a man you can't find when you want. And Williams – I ain't see him for a long time, because he owe me a pound and he don't come my way these days.'

'Still,' Roy say, 'we will have to manage to get a side together. If we back out of this now them English fellars will say we are only talkers. You better wait for me after work this evening, and we will go around by some of the boys and see what we could do.'

That was the Monday, and the Wednesday night about twelve of the boys get together in Algernon room in Kensal

Rise, and Algernon boiling water in the kettle and making tea while they discuss the situation.

'Algernon always have big mouth, and at last it land him in trouble.'

'Cricket! I never play in my life!'

'I uses to play a little "pass-out" in my days, but to go and play against a English side! Boy, them fellars like this game, and they could play, too!'

'One time I hit a ball and it went over a fence and break a lady window and . . .'

'All right, all right, ease up on the good old days, the problem is right now. I mean, we have to rally.'

'Yes, and then when we go there everybody get bowl for duck, and when them fellars batting we can't get them out. Not me.'

But in the end, after a lot of blague and argument, they agree that they would go and play.

'What about some practice?' Wilky say anxiously. Wilky was the only fellar who really serious about the game.

'Practice!' Roy say. 'It ain't have time for that. I wonder if I could still hold a bat?' And he get up and pick up a stick Algernon had in the corner and begin to make stance.

'Is not that way to hold a bat, stupid. Is so.'

And there in Algernon room the boys begin to remember what they could of the game, and Wilky saying he ain't playing unless he is captain, and Eric saying he ain't playing unless he get pads because one time a cork ball nearly break his shinbone, and a fellar name Chips pull a cricket cap from his back pocket and trying it on in front a mirror.

So everything was arranged in a half-hearted sort of way. When the great day come, Algernon had hopes that they might postpone the match, because only eight of the boys turn up, but the English captain say it was a shame for them to return without playing, that he would make his side eight, too.

Well that Saturday on the village green was a historic day. Whether cold feet take the English side because of the licks the West Indies eleven was sharing at Lord's I can't say, but the fact is that they had to bowl first and they only coming down with some nice hop-and-drop that the boys lashing for six and four.

When Algernon turn to bat he walk out like a veteran. He bend down and inspect the pitch closely and shake his head, as if he ain't too satisfied with the condition of it but had to put up with it. He put on gloves, stretch out his hands as if he about to shift a heavy tyre in the factory, and take up the most unorthodox stance them English fellars ever did see. Algernon legs wide apart as if he doing the split and he have the bat already swing over his shoulder although the bowler ain't bowl yet. The umpire making sign to him that he covering the wicket but Algernon do as if he can't see. He make up his mind that he rather go for l.b.w. than for the stumps to fly.

No doubt an ordinary ball thrown with ease would have had him out in two-twos, but as I was saying, it look as if the unusual play of the boys have the Englishers in a quandary, and the bowler come down with a nice hop-and-drop that a baby couldn't miss.

Algernon close his eyes and he make a swipe at the ball, and he swipe so hard that when the bat collide the ball went right out of the field and fall in the road.

Them Englishers never see a stroke like that in their lives. All heads turn up to the sky watching the ball going.

Algernon feel like a king: only thing, when he hit the ball the bat went after it and nearly knock down a English fellar who was fielding silly-mid-on-square-leg.

Well praise the lord, the score was then sixty-nine and one set of rain start to fall and stop the match.

Later on, entertaining the boys in the local pub, the Englishers asking all sort of questions, like why they stand so and so and why they make such and such a stroke, and the boys talking as if cricket so common in the West Indies that the babies born either with a bat or a ball, depending on if it would be a good bowler or batsman.

'That was a wonderful shot,' Charles tell Algernon grudgingly. Charles still had a feeling that the boys was only talkers, but so much controversy raging that he don't know what to say.

'If my bat didn't fly out my hand,' Algernon say, and wave his hand in the air dramatically, as if to say he would have lost the ball in the other county.

'Of course, we still have to see your bowling,' the English captain say. 'Pity about the rain – usual English weather, you know.'

'Bowling!' Algernon echo, feeling as if he is a Walcott and a Valentine roll into one. 'Oh yes, we must come back some time and finish off the match.'

'What about next Saturday?' the captain press, eager to see the boys in action again, not sure if he was dreaming about all them wild swipe and crazy strokes.

'Sure, I'll get the boys together,' Algernon say.

Algernon say that, but it wasn't possible, because none of them wanted to go back after batting, frighten that they won't be able to bowl the Englishers out.

And Charles keep reminding Algernon all the time, but Algernon keep saying how the boys scatter about, some gone Birmingham to live, and others move and gone to work somewhere else, and he can't find them anywhere.

'Never mind,' Algernon tell Charles, 'next cricket season I will get a sharp eleven together and come down your way for another match. Now, if you want me to show you how I make that stroke . . .'

Obeah in the Grove

DOWN BY Ladbroke Grove – and I don't mean the posh part near to Holland Park, but when you start to go west: the more west you go, the more worse things get – it have a certain street, and a certain house, and in front the house have a plane tree, and one day if you pass there and you look up in the plane tree, you will see a green bottle dangling on a piece of twine, and a big bone stick up between two branch. It had a lot of other things there, and a chain of beads, but they fall down: the chain get burst and the beads scatter all about and get lost.

You want to know what them things doing up in that tree, eh? Well, I will tell you. I mean, in the West Indies, from the time you see thing like that, you know right away that some-body in for something, because thing like that mean black magic and obeah. Sometimes in the islands you get up in the morning please God and you stretch and yawn, and when you look by your window you see some bird feather, or a piece of cloth, and right away you know that somebody trying to work a zeppy on you, somebody calling evil spirits on your head. When you look by your doorstep you see as if somebody throw a bucket of blood down there. Is time then to take steps right away to turn the evil aside, or else before you know what happening all sorts of things begin to happen, like you trip and fall down and break your hand, or else the house catch fire, or you lose your job or something. One time even it happen to a fellar that he start to swell as if he pregnant, and doctors or nobody could do anything, and everybody thought this man was going to have a baby. But that is another ballad.

Now, the latest rake when them English landlord and landlady want to sell house, is to get the tenants out, because the more empty room they have the more money they could ask for the place. And to get the tenants out, what some of them was doing was to let out rooms to spades, and when the white tenants see that they say: 'Gracious me! I can't stay in this house any longer!' and they hustle to get another room while the landlord laughing. Next thing, he give the spades notice, and by the time he ready to sell house bam! the whole house empty.

In fact, this rake was so successful that if any landlord have undesirable white tenants, the best thing was to let out couple of rooms to coloured people, and one by one the Nordics would evacuate. They used to do that, especially in them houses what have tenants from long before the war, who paying ten-twelve shillings for two-three rooms, because these days, you only have to put a put-you-up and a table and two chairs in a room and hit somebody three-four guineas a week for it.

Well this house in the Grove that I telling you about was old, I mean real old, with the paint peeling off and the roof leaking and sometimes though the sun shining the walls oozing water like a spring.

'When are we going to move,' the wife asking the man every day, 'the house will fall about our heads one day.'

'We won't get much for the place with all the flats occupied,' the man grumble.

'Jack told you what to do,' the wife say. 'Let us move out from these two rooms we have, and rent them to coloured people. Jack said when he did that, in a short time all the tenants moved and he didn't have any trouble.'

'You think Bill and Agnes will like that?' the man say. He was talking about two of the tenants: every Saturday night he and Bill used to go in the pub to play darts and drink mild and bitter, while the wife and Agnes sit down in a corner with two big glass of brown ale and gossip.

'We don't have to tell anybody anything,' the wife say. 'See how much money Jack is making these days, charging two guineas for a room that he used to get ten shillings for at one time. If even we don't get the house sold, we will be able to get good rent for the rooms.'

The very next day the wife went and put a notice up in an advertisement window by the tube station, saying that coloured people were welcome. As luck would have it, same day Agnes was passing there on the way to the Bendix with dirty clothes, and she stop by the notice board to read. I mean, it have people like that, who ain't looking for anything in particular, but they just like to stand up near them notice board and read.

'Good gracious me!' Agnes gasp when she see the address, 'that's where I live!' and she nearly drop the bag of dirty clothes.

When she get back home she went to the wife and the wife say yes. The wife say, why shouldn't we be broad-minded, these people see so much trouble to get a place to live, we shouldn't discriminate, after all, what's wrong with coloured people. And in fact the wife outdid herself explaining to Agnes after Agnes sniff and went away, the wife stand there amazed at her own loquacity about the rights of human beings.

When the husband come home from work she tell him how Agnes take alarm and she say: 'It will work like a charm.'

She wouldn't have said that if she knew about the charm the boys was going to throw on the house in the end.

The Sunday morning, four of the boys was looking for place. They walk all the way from Paddington station reading notice board, until they land up in the Grove. The boys was Fiji, Algernon, Winky and Buttards, and all of them come from Jamaica.

Winky take a second look at the notice.

'That don't look so bad,' he say.

'It always have a catch when they say coloured people welcome,' Fiji say.

'Well we could go and see the joint,' Algernon say.

First they pass the house, giving it a once-over as they pass by.

'This house don't look good,' Algernon say.

'Is a wonder it still standing up,' Buttards say.

They turn around and start to walk again to the house.

'You go Algernon,' Winky say.

'No, you go Winky,' Algernon say.

Same time Agnes come out to go by the tube station to buy the *Pictorial* and *News of the World*, and Fiji call out 'Good morning . . .' but Agnes only sniff and pass them like a full No. 15.

'Go and ask for the landlord, man,' Buttards say, not addressing anyone in particular.

The four of them march up to the door and ring the bell. The wife come out, and as soon as she see the boys she fling the door open wide.

'Come in, come in,' she say, as if she greeting distant relatives she ain't see for a long time, and before the boys could say anything she leading them to the vacant rooms.

Well in the end the boys move in. Atmosphere tense in the house, the other tenants won't even say good morning or how do you do: in fact, in that first week two of them manage to find another place and shift out from the Grove.

'A few weeks more,' the wife tell the husband, 'and we'll be rid of them all.'

One night Buttards was having a quick one in the pub when Bill come up to him.

'You are one of the chaps living where I stay,' he say.

'Yes,' Buttards say, and wanting to make friends, he say, 'what you having?'

'Nothing,' Bill say shortly. 'But I want to tell you something. That house is going to be sold, the owner only took you coloured chaps in to get rid of us.'

And Bill leave Buttards to cogitate on those words.

Buttards cogitate, and went home to tell the boys what the position was, and then all of them start to cogitate.

'You see how it is in this country,' Buttards start to moan.

'I wasn't so keen to come here in the first place,' Winky say.

'And to think the landlady so nice to us,' Algernon say.

Only Fiji keeping quiet, and when they ask him what he have to say, he still ain't saying nothing, just sit down there working the old brains. Well when you see Fiji serious and meditating, something in the air, something brewing, and if you not Fiji friend you best hads look out, because sometimes some wild kind of plan does come to Fiji when he cogitating like that, and nothing don't stop him from doing what he plan to do.

After dinner in the evening it look like Fiji relax a little on the brain, and Winky was anxious to find out what Fiji was thinking about, so he ask him: 'What is the plan?'

'The plan is this. Take it easy, don't let them know that we know anything. In fact, treat the landlady and she husband real good, make it a real calm before the storm.'

'And what is the storm?' Buttards ask.

'The storm is this,' Fiji say, helping himself to Winky's Woods. 'We will work a little zeppy on the house. Just a little thing. Nothing much. The roof might fall in. The walls might cave in. The flooring might drop out. The whole house might tumble down one night as if the vengeance of Moko hit it. Nothing much.'

'Boy, we not back home in Jamaica now, you know,' Winky say. Winky seeing this old house falling down on him when he sleeping and he frighten.

'But what happen in Jamaica could happen here,' Fiji say.

'You mean a little obeah?' Algernon say the word at last.

'I mean a little obeah,' Fiji say after Algernon. 'Now, all of we in this together, right?'

'Right,' the others say.

'Good. Leave everything to me.'

Well in the next few days, the wife and she husband wondering what happen to the boys, they getting on so nice.
When the wife going to clean out the rooms, the boys won't
let her do a stroke of work. When she want to change the
sheets, the boys saying is all right, they would launder the
sheets themselves, she mustn't worry about a thing. Winky
went so far as to buy a bunch of daffodil one evening and
bring home and give to the landlady.

'Those coloured chaps must suspect something,' the wife say.

'It's just like them to try and make up to us,' the man say.

Two weeks later a big parcel come for Fiji from Jamaica. By
this time everybody who white clear out of the house, and
only the boys remain, with two weeks' notice hanging over
their heads. In fact, the owner done have the house in the
hands of a agent for sale.

'Ah, like you get something from home,' the others say to
Fiji when he come home and was opening the parcel.

'I hope is pepper sauce,' Winky say.

Fiji ain't say nothing, he just open the parcel and start to
take out some things one by one. When the boys see what it is
that Fiji taking out, they back away.

'You know how to deal with those things, Fiji?' Buttards
ask in a scared voice.

'Sure,' Fiji say. 'Ain't I say leave it to me? Now, Algernon,
you went to see that place in Acton?'

'Yes,' Algernon say. 'Is all right, we could move in on the
Saturday.'

'Good. Tomorrow is Friday. I not going to work. Tell the
landlady I not feeling well and don't want no interruptions
while I am resting. When you all come back in the evening,
I will be ready. We can't afford to waste time with these things
else they mightn't work.'

The next day Fiji lock himself up in the room, and stay
there all day with the things he get from Jamaica. Once the
landlady pass near the door and she hear as if Fiji talking to

himself or singing or chanting or something, and she smell a smell as if somebody burning incense. But she ain't pay no particular attention.

When all the boys was home in the evening Fiji begin to give them instructions.

'Winky, you finish all the packing, because we have to pull out of here early in the morning – I not sure when this obeah would start to work, so we better clear out as soon as we could. Algernon, you see this here? Tonight when you get a chance, I want you to hide it over the front door – it have a ledge there. And this other thing, put it over the back door. Hide them good, so nobody won't see unless they climb up and look on the ledge. Buttards, you and I have to do the main thing'.

Fiji went to the window and open it. It had a branch of the plane tree what was near the window.

'You see that branch?' Fiji ask Buttards, 'you think you could climb up on the tree from this window?'

'I don't know about these trees in London,' Buttards start to get cagey. 'Them branch might be weak and brittle.'

'English trees is the strongest trees,' Fiji say. 'You never hear about hearts of oak?'

'What you want me to climb that tree for?'

'I want you to put some things in it. Not now, mind you. Midnight time, when nobody could see.'

Well everything went into execution that night as Fiji plan, though Buttards nearly fall down from the tree climbing in the dark, as Fiji wanted him to go to the top branch. And early the next morning the boys pull out for this other place in Acton, Fiji glancing up in the tree as they pass to make sure Buttards place all the things correctly.

Now you and me ain't going to argue about obeah. I have other things to do, and I only want to give you the episode how it happen.

Four people in all come to see the house to buy it, but all of them went away: in fact, a week later one of them was mad. Then the walls start to crack, the roof falling down bit by bit, the concrete steps under the tree in the front start to crumble. All this happening in a matter of days, mind you. Like one day the wife walking up the stairs to go to the top flat and the stairs break down and she break she foot, and the next day the husband was opening the front door and the whole door come away and nearly knock him down, and the day after that he hear that he lose his job.

The house get a kind of look about it, people afraid to even pass near it in the street. True a lot of the houses in London like that, but this one as if it threatening to collapse any minute. The landlady and she husband had was to move out and get furnished rooms, and the agent say he washing his hands of the matter, that it look as if the house have a jinx, that nobody want to buy it.

Well, is winter now and all the leaves fall off the trees, so if by chance you ever liming in the Grove and you want to see for yourself, just go in that certain street. You can't miss the house at all, and you will see that bottle dangling from the top branch where Buttards nearly fall down when he was putting it there in the dark.

Only thing, mind and don't pass too near, 'cause that house have the vengeance of Moko on it and it might tumble down any time.

Basement Lullaby

IN A DINGY basement room in Paddington what the health authorities warn the landlord not to rent without renovating, Bar 20 and Fred was laying down after an all-night session in the West End. Every night is all-night session for them, because the two of them working in a band in a club, and when they get back home in the morning they hitting the hay real hard.

But this morning as if a kind of restlessness possess Bar 20.

'Fred?'

'Um?'

'You see that girl who come in the club about ten o'clock?'

'What girl?'

'The one with the American army officer. I think I see that girl somewhere before. I not sure, but I would swear to God I see she liming out on the Bayswater road one night.'

'Um.'

'From the Bayswater road to a Park Lane night club is a big jump.'

'All right, all right, is a big jump, so what?'

The wall-paper on the walls of the room coming off and hanging down like drapery: where it staying put, is because the landlord fix it with scotch tape. The wood panelling have crack and it hollow inside where woodworms on a rampage. The ceiling have so much crack that it look like a map of a country what only have rivers and lakes. The light of the good day shut out of this room as if is an evil place.

'Fred.'

'Um?'

'I don't too like this work, you know. More than a year now, every night we playing in that club, and it get so I don't know what it like when is day, because we does be always sleeping. You know how long I ain't seen the sun? You sleep all day, then you get up eight o'clock in the evening and go to work, and come back five-six o'clock in the morning. I don't like it, Fred. It ain't natural.'

'Um.'

The dilapidation of the room accented by the state the boys have it in. From the time he get in Bar 20 does throw his clothes all about, on the ground, on the chairs, on the table, and make a kind of wild dive for the bed. On the table, it have a pack of twenty Players that open, two bottles of Scotch whisky, and both of them open, and two glasses. It have a piano push up in one corner of the room, and some music sheets scatter over it.

Fred emitting some deep cough now and then, and pulling the blanket over his head and stirring restlessly, trying hard to fall asleep.

Bar 20 lay there with his hands clasped behind his head, and his knees up with legs crossed, like how sometimes in them films they show you the star-boy lay down there thinking.

'Fred.'

'What?'

'We have a lot of money save up man, is time we look for another place to live. One day we must go and look for place. We paying three pounds here, and I sure we could get a better place for that.'

'Um.'

'You know, you still ain't got the melody right in that new calypso. Last night you make the same mistake again. Still, I suppose them English people won't know the difference.'

Bar 20 get up and pour a drink. 'You want a drink?' he ask Fred.

'Uh-uh.'

Bar 20 drink and went and lay down again.

Outside, smog piling up and creeping down to the basement and coming through the chink in the window. The atmosphere in the room hazy.

Fred cough and Bar 20 say: 'You best hads go to see a doctor about that cough.'

Fred roll over on the other side. Though he ain't asleep yet, he keeping his eyes shut tight and trying to will himself to doze off.

'Fred?'

'What the arse?'

'Fred, how much is £75,000 in West Indian dollars?'

As Fred didn't answer Bar 20 try to work it out himself but give up, grumbling: 'A man even forget how to multiply! But still, is a lot of money. What and what I wouldn't do with that money! You know, I wonder how many West Indians sit down like this and think the same way?' He cast a quick look at Fred. Fred back turn: his bottom pushing against the blanket.

'Fred, you sleeping?'

'Um.'

'Listen, I had a message for you that I forget. Dorothy say you must phone her this morning. She say is important. You hearing?'

'Um.'

'Well don't say I didn't tell you, eh. She sound as if she out for your head. But don't let her pull anything on you: I get a niggergram she was in Piccadilly the other night with a English fellar.'

Bar 20 get up again and light a cigarette. 'You want a cigarette?'

'No thanks.'

Bar 20 look around the room restlessly. He spot a airmail letter that the landlord did push under the door. He pick it up and went back on the bed and lay down and read.

'Big things happening home, boy!' he say, reading the letter. 'The Americans taking over all the oilfields, and my sister say things just like it was during the war, with Yankee dollar flowing all about the place.' He commented on this bit of news: 'This country too cheap, they allow the Americans to buy all the oil and run the show, how they expect to keep the colonies like that?'

For an instant Fred showed his head above the blanket and glared hatefully with red, bleary eyes at Bar 20, but Bar 20 wasn't looking.

'A-a, you know who dead? Mussolini! You remember Mussolini? The one-foot fellar what used to sell newspaper by the library corner in San Fernando? A car knock him down in Coffee street, and he dead before they could take him hospital.'

Bar 20 begin to scratch his legs, and he lean back comfortably on the pillow and finish reading the letter. The news from home make him homesick.

'Fred?'

'Jesus Christ!'

'Fred, the family having some trouble back home with the cocoa estate – it look as if a kind of blight attack the trees . . .'

'Listen man.' Fred prop himself up on an elbow and turn to Bar 20. 'What the arse happen to you this morning? Here we is in London, in London, man, three-four thousand miles from home, and you decide to talk about the library corner in San Fernando and the cocoa estate. What happen? You ain't sleepy today? You didn't work enough last night, or what?' And Fred roll over and cover himself with the blanket, and crouch up in an S with his hands clasped between his knees.

All the sounds of the outside world unheard in that basement room. Even sounds in the house can't be heard: is as if down there the two boys cut away from life. This was the regular situation, but this morning as if Bar 20 become aware of it for the first time.

'Fred?'

'What is it this time?'

'As if the whole world dead, eh, you can't hear anything down here in the basement. Life in London really different from back home, boy. Imagine how we here, living under the earth, with the street above our heads! If you tell them so in Trinidad they laugh at you, they want to know if you living in a hole or what ...'

'Bar 20, you really —ing up a good time, yes. What happen to you this morning? Why, of all mornings, you choosing this one? Jesus, man, I trying to sleep. S-l-e-e-p. You know what that mean? Take ease, old man, take ease.'

'But if the telephone ring, you can't hear it,' Bar 20 went on. 'Suppose Dorothy ring up, how you will know? Down here like the Black Hole of Calcutta. We must really move.'

'Um.'

'Why you open the other bottle of whisky? Now both bottles open.'

'Listen,' Fred say, propping up on his elbow again, 'why you don't go and take some fresh air? Go for a walk in the park or something?'

'In all that smog?' Bar 20 say. 'You must be mad!'

'I am begging you,' Fred say as softly as he could, 'keep quiet and sleep. You not getting enough sleep these days, that's why you not handling the drums well. You talking about me not getting the melody right, but I notice the drums not keeping up with the rest of the band these nights.'

'What you talking about?' Bar 20 say. 'Man, I playing the drums right ...'

'Yes, yes,' Fred say quickly. 'But we go talk about it later.'

Fred move up close to the wall, getting as far away from Bar 20 as he could, and disappear under the blanket.

Bar 20 begin to read the letter again, pretending that is the first time he seeing it. After that, he get up and went and had another drink. Then he pick up his trousers and push his hand in the pocket and begin to check how much money he have. A two-and-six fall and roll. Bar 20 dive for it, and collide with a leg of the table. One bottle of whisky fall and hit the other one, and the two of them roll off the table and break up on the ground. Good Scotch whisky running like water on the floor.

'Fred?'

Fred keep quiet.

'Oh hell,' Bar 20 say, but this time his voice a lot quieter, as if he frighten for the damage that he cause. He watch the whisky flowing zig-zag for a minute. Then he went and lay down on the bed, as quiet as a mouse.

Fred wait for about fifteen minutes, until he was sure that Bar 20 dropping off into a nice sleep.

Then he get up and put on all the lights in the room, and turn on the radio full blast. He went to the piano and start to pound out a calypso number, stamping his foot hard to keep time.

'What the hell you doing, Fred?' Bar 20 leap up in bed at the sudden din.

'I playing you a lullaby,' Fred say, hoping he could keep it up until he drive Bar 20 mad.

My Girl and the City

ALL THESE WORDS that I hope to write, I have written them already many times in my mind. I have had many beginnings, each as good or as bad as the other. Hurtling in the underground from station to station, mind the doors, missed it!, there is no substitute for wool: waiting for a bus in Piccadilly Circus: walking across Waterloo bridge: watching the bed of the Thames when the tide is out – choose one, choose a time, a place, any time or any place, and take off, as if this were interrupted conversation, as if you and I were earnest friends and there is no need for preliminary remark.

One day of any day it is like this. I wait for my girl on Waterloo bridge, and when she comes there is a mighty wind blowing across the river, and we lean against it and laugh, her skirt skylarking, her hair whipping across her face.

I wooed my girl, mostly on her way home from work, and I talked a great deal. Often, it was as if I had never spoken, I heard my words echo in deep caverns of thought, as if they hung about like cigarette smoke in a still room, missionless; or else they were lost for ever in the sounds of the city.

We used to wait for a 196 under the railway bridge across the Waterloo road. There were always long queues and it looked like we would never get a bus. Fidgeting in that line of impatient humanity I got in precious words edgeways, and a train would rumble and drown my words in thundering steel. Still, it was important to talk. In the crowded bus, as if I wooed three or four instead of one, I shot words over my shoulder, across seats; once past a bespectacled man reading the *Evening*

News who lowered his paper and eyed me that I was mad. My words bumped against people's faces, on the glass window of the bus; they found passage between 'fares please' and once I got to writing things on a piece of paper and pushing my hand over two seats.

The journey ended there was urgent need to communicate before we parted.

All these things I say, I said, waving my hand in the air as if to catch the words floating about me and give them mission. I say them because I want you to know, I don't ever want to regret afterwards that I didn't say enough, I would rather say too much.

Take that Saturday evening, I am waiting for her in Victoria station. When she comes we take the Northern Line to Belsize Park (I know a way to the heath from there, I said). When we get out of the lift and step outside there is a sudden downpour and everyone scampers back into the station. We wait a while, then go out in it. We get lost. I say, Let us ask that fellow the way. But she says No, fancy asking someone the way to the heath on this rainy night, just find out how to get back to the tube station.

We go back, I get my bearings afresh, and we set off. She is hungry. Wait here, I say under a tree at the side of the road, and I go to a pub for some sandwiches. Water slips off me and makes puddles on the counter as I place my order. The man is taking a long time and I go to the door and wave to her across the street signifying I shan't be too long.

When I go out she has crossed the road and is sheltering in a doorway pouting. You leave me standing in the rain and stay such a long time, she says. I had to wait for the sandwiches, I say, what do you think, I was having a quick one? Yes, she says.

We walk on through the rain and we get to the heath and the rain is falling slantways and carefree and miserable. For a minute we move around in an indecisive way as if we're looking for some particular spot. Then we see a tree which might offer some shelter and we go there and sit on a bench wet and bedraggled.

I am sorry for all this rain, I say, as if I were responsible I take off her raincoat and make her put on my quilted jacket. She takes off her soaking shoes and tucks her feet under her skirt on the bench. She tries to dry her hair with a handkerchief. I offer her the sandwiches and light a cigarette for myself. Go on, have one, she says. I take a half and munch it, and smoke.

It is cold there. The wind is raging in the leaves of the trees, and the rain is pelting. But abruptly it ceases, the clouds break up in the sky, and the moon shines. When the moon shines, it shines on her face, and I look at her, the beauty of her washed by rain, and I think many things.

Suddenly we are kissing and I wish I could die there and then and there's an end to everything, to all the Jesus-Christ thoughts that make up every moment of my existence.

Writing all this now – and some weeks have gone by since I started – it is lifeless and insipid and useless. Only at the time, there was something, a thought that propelled me. Always, in looking back, there was something, and at the time I am aware of it, and the creation goes on and on in my mind while I look at all the faces around me in the tube, the restless rustle of newspapers, the hiss of air as the doors close, the enaction of life in a variety of form.

Once I told her and she said, as she was a stenographer, that she would come with me and we would ride the Inner Circle and I would just voice my thoughts and she would write them down, and that way we could make something of it. Once the train was crowded and she sat opposite to me and after a while I looked at her and she smiled and turned away. What is all this, what is the meaning of all these things that happen to people, the movement from one place to another, lighting a cigarette, slipping a coin into a slot and pulling a drawer for chocolate, buying a return ticket, waiting for a bus, working the crossword puzzle in the *Evening Standard*?

Sometimes you are in the underground and you have no idea what the weather is like, and the train shoots out of a tunnel and sunlight floods you, falls across your newspaper, makes the passengers squint and look up.

There is a face you have for sitting at home and talking, there is a face you have for working in the office, there is a face, a bearing, a demeanour for each time and place. There is above all a face for travelling, and when you have seen one you have seen all. In a rush hour, when we are breathing down each other's neck, we look at each other and glance quickly away. There is not a great deal to look at in the narrow confines of a carriage except people, and the faces of people, but no one deserves a glass of Hall's wine more than you do. We justle in the subway from train to lift, we wait, shifting our feet. When we are all herded inside we hear the footsteps of a straggler for whom the operator waits, and we try to figure out what sort of a footstep it is, if he feels the lift will wait for him; we are glad if he is left waiting while we shoot upward. Out of the lift, down the street, up the road: in ten seconds flat it is over, and we have to begin again.

One morning I am coming into the city by the night bus 287 from Streatham. It is after one o'clock; I have been stranded again after seeing my girl home. When we get to Westminster bridge the sky is marvellously clear with a few stray patches of beautiful cloud among which stars sparkle. The moon stands over Waterloo bridge, above the Houses of Parliament sharply outlined, and it throws gold on the waters of the Thames. The Embankment is quiet, only a few people loiter around the public convenience near to the Charing Cross underground which is open all night. A man sleeps on a bench. His head is resting under headlines: Suez Deadlock.

Going back to that same spot about five o'clock in the evening, there was absolutely nothing to recall the atmosphere of the early morning hours. Life had taken over completely, and there was nothing but people. People waiting for buses, people hustling for trains.

I go to Waterloo bridge and they come pouring out of the offices and they bob up and down as they walk across the bridge. From the station green trains come and go relentlessly. Motion mesmerises me into immobility. There are lines of motion across the river, on the river.

Sometimes we sat on a bench near the river, and if the tide was out you could see the muddy bed of the river and the swans grubbing. Such spots, when found, are pleasant to loiter in. Sitting in one of those places – choose one, and choose a time – where it is possible to escape for a brief spell from Christ and the cup of tea, I have known a great frustration and weariness. All these things, said, have been said before, the river seen, the skirt pressed against the swelling thigh noted, the lunch hour eating apples in the sphinx's lap under Cleopatra's Needle observed and duly registered: even to talk of the frustration is a repetition. What am I to do, am I to take each circumstance, each thing seen, noted, and mill them in my mind and spit out something entirely different from the reality?

My girl is very real. She hated the city, I don't know why. It's like that sometimes, a person doesn't have to have a reason. A lot of people don't like London that way, you ask them why and they shrug, and a shrug is sometimes a powerful reply to a question.

She shrugged when I asked her why, and when she asked me why I loved London I too shrugged. But after a minute I thought I would try to explain, because too a shrug is an easy way out of a lot of things.

Falteringly I told her how one night it was late and I found a fish and chips shop open in the East End and I bought and ate in the dark street walking; and of the cup of tea in an all-night café in Kensington one grim winter morning; and

of the first time I ever queued in this country in '50 to see the
Swan Lake ballet, and the friend who was with me gave a
busker two and six because he was playing Sentimental Journey on a mouth-organ.

But why do you love London, she said.

You can't talk about a thing like that, not really. Maybe I
could have told her because one evening in the summer I was
waiting for her, only it wasn't like summer at all. Rain had
been falling all day, and a haze hung about the bridges across
the river, and the water was muddy and brown, and there was
a kind of wistfulness and sadness about the evening. The way
St Paul's was, half-hidden in the rain, the motionless trees
along the Embankment. But you say a thing like that and
people don't understand at all. How sometimes a surge of
greatness could sweep over you when you see something.

But even if I had said all that and much more, it would not
have been what I meant. You could be lonely as hell in the
city, then one day you look around you and you realise everybody else is lonely too, withdrawn, locked, rushing home out
of the chaos: blank faces, unseeing eyes, millions and millions
of them, up the Strand, down the Strand, jostling in Charing
Cross for the 5.20: in Victoria station, a pretty continental girl
wearing a light, becoming shade of lipstick stands away from
the board on which the departure of trains appear and cocks
her head sideways, hands thrust into pockets of a fawn raincoat.

I catch the eyes of this girl with my own: we each register
sight, appreciation: we look away, our eyes pick up casual
station activities: she turns to an automatic refreshment machine, hesitant, not sure if she would be able to operate it.

Things happen, and are finished with for ever: I did not talk
to her, I did not look her way again, or even think of her.

I look on the wall of the station at the clock, it is after half-
past eight, and my girl was to have met me since six o'clock.
I feel in my pockets for pennies to telephone. I only have two.
I ask change of a stander with the usual embarrassment: when

I telephone, the line is engaged. I alternate between standing in the spot we have arranged to meet and telephoning, but each time the line is engaged. I call the exchange: they ascertain that something is wrong with the line.

At ten minutes to nine I am eating a cornedbeef sandwich when she comes. Suddenly now nothing matters except that she is here. She never expected that I would still be waiting, but she came on the offchance. I never expected that she would come, but I waited on the offchance.

Now I have a different word for this thing that happened – an offchance, but that does not explain why it happens, and what it is that really happens. We go to St James's Park, we sit under a tree, we kiss, the moon can be seen between leaves.

Wooing my way towards, sometimes in our casual conversation we came near to great, fundamental truths, and it was a little frightening. It wasn't like wooing at all, it was more discussion of when will it end, and must it ever end, and how did it begin, and how go on from here? We scattered words on the green summer grass, under trees, on dry leaves in a wood of quivering aspens, and sometimes it was as if I was struck speechless with too much to say, and held my tongue between thoughts frightened of utterance.

Once again I am on a green train returning to the heart from the suburbs, and I look out of window into windows of private lives flashed on my brain. Bread being sliced, a man taking off a jacket, an old woman knitting. And all these things I see – the curve of a woman's arm, undressing, the blankets being tucked, and once a solitary figure staring at trains as I stared at windows. All the way into London Bridge – is falling down, is falling down, the wheels say: one must have a thought – where buildings and the shadows of them encroach on the railway tracks. Now the train crawls across the bridges, dark steel in the darkness: the thoughtful gloom of Waterloo: Charing Cross bridge, Thames reflecting lights, and the silhouettes of city buildings against the sky of the night.

When I was in New York, many times I went into that city late at night after a sally to the outskirts, it lighted up with a million lights, but never a feeling as on entering London. Each return to the city is loaded with thought, so that by the time I take the Inner Circle I am as light as air.

At last I think I know what it is all about. I move around in a world of words. Everything that happens is words. But pure expression is nothing. One must build on the things that happen: it is insufficient to say I sat in the underground and the train hurtled through the darkness and someone isn't using Amplex. So what? So now I weave, I say there was an old man on whose face wrinkles rivered, whose hands were shapeful with arthritis but when he spoke, oddly enough, his voice was young and gay.

But there was no old man, there was nothing, and there is never ever anything.

My girl, she is beautiful to look at. I have seen her in sunlight and in moonlight, and her face carves an exquisite shape in darkness.

These things we talk, I burst out, why mustn't I say them? If I love you, why shouldn't I tell you so?

I love London, she said.

Other titles by Sam Selvon in the Longman Caribbean Writers Series

A Brighter Sun

This major first novel by one of the Caribbean's greatest playwrights is a sensitively drawn picture of Trinidadian life in the turbulent years of the Second World War.

A first novel of remarkable quality...a poetic, amusing and frequently touching portrait of a community. Times Literary Supplement.

0 582 64265 5

The Lonely Londoners

The definitive novel about London's West Indians Financial Times.

A striking account of the waves of West Indians who arrived in London in the 1950s in search of a prosperous future. Instead they are faced with a cool reception and the harsh realities of living hand to mouth, of racism, bone-chilling weather and bleak prospects. Yet friendships flourish and in time they learn to survive.

The unforgettable picaresque 'The Lonely Londoners', a vernacular comedy of pathos. The Gurdian.

0 582 64264 7

Longman Caribbean Writers

Title	Author	ISBN
Satellite City	A McKenzie	0 582 08688 4
Karl and Other Stories	V Pollard	0 582 22726 7
Homestretch	V Pollard	0 582 22732 1
Discoveries	J Wickham	0 582 21804 7
Chieftain's Carnival	M Anthony	0 582 21805 5
DreamStories	K Brathwaite	0 582 09340 6
Arrival of the Snakewoman	O Senior	0 582 03170 2
Summer Lightning	O Senior	0 582 78627 4
The Dragon Can't Dance	E Lovelace	0 582 64231 0
Ways of Sunlight	S Selvon	0 582 64261 2
The Lonely Londoners	S Selvon	0 582 64264 7
A Brighter Sun	S Selvon	0 582 64265 5
Foreday Morning	S Selvon	0 582 03982 7
In the Castle of my Skin	G Lamming	0 582 64267 1
My Bones and My Flute	E Mittelholzer	0 582 78552 9
Black Albino	N Roy	0 582 78563 4
The Children of Sisyphus	O Patterson	0 582 78571 5
The Jumbie Bird	I Khan	0 582 78619 3
Plays for Today	E Hill *et al*	0 582 78620 7
Old Story Time and Smile Orange	T.D. Rhone	0 582 78633 9
Baby Mother and the King of Swords	L Goodison	0 582 05492 3
Two Roads to Mount Joyful	E McKenzie	0 582 07125 9
Voiceprint	S Brown *et al*	0 582 78629 0

All these titles are available or can be ordered from your local book-seller. For further information on these titles, and on study guides available, contact your local Longman agent or Longman International Education, Longman Group Limited, Longman House, Burnt Mill, Harlow, Essex, CM20 2JE, England.